The Democratic Moment

The Democratic Moment

South Africa's Prospects under Jacob Zuma

by
Xolela Mangcu

First published by Jacana Media (Pty) Ltd in 2009

10 Orange Street
Sunnyside
Auckland Park 2092
South Africa
+2711 628 3200
www.jacana.co.za

ISBN 978-1-77009-774-2

Set in Ehrhardt 11/15pt
Printed by CTP Book Printers
ISO 12647 compliant

Job No. 001066

See a complete list of Jacana titles at www.jacana.co.za

To my children, for the love and joy they bring

Contents

Prologue 1

Introduction 7

1. Elite fear of democracy: a historical perspective 13

2. 'We will kill for Zuma': militarism as the new politics of
   authenticity 32

3. Politics as law, law as politics: the different cases of
   Jacob Zuma and John Hlophe 53

4. The limits of the cultural aesthetic of liberal modernity:
   how the media were compromised 86

5. Congress of the what? Prospects for opposition politics 113

6. Making government responsive: historical, symbolic and
   institutional imagination 134

7. Building active citizenship at home and abroad: towards a
   transatlantic alliance on active citizenship 165

Conclusion: The next big battle for leadership 186

Index 193

Acknowledgements

I should like to thank the Vice-Chancellor of the University of Johannesburg, Ihron Rensburg, the Deputy Vice-Chancellor (Research, Innovation and Advancement), Adam Habib, and the Executive Director for Advancement, Kerry Swift, for providing me with the intellectual space for writing this book. Thanks also go to political analyst Mcebisi Ndletyana for reading draft manuscripts of the book, and to Emelda Manjezi, Ayanda Msibi and Ingrid van Niekerk for their administrative support.

I am grateful to the editors of the *Sunday Times*, *Business Day* and *The Weekender*, and the *Mail & Guardian* for allowing me to reproduce in this book some of my columns which appeared in their newspapers.

Xolela Mangcu

Prologue

My children have been impatiently asking me when the sequel to my previous book, *To the Brink*, would be coming out. As with *Harry Potter*, books must have sequels. They even suggested the design and colour of the cover. *To the Brink* was red; this one must be yellow. Now if you are a parent, you will know how hard it can be to disappoint children and somehow make up for it. The disappointing news is that this is *not* a sequel to the previous book. You can read the two together, but to explain the rise of Jacob Zuma in terms of Thabo Mbeki would be to deny the latter a break and the former a new start. To be sure, it is impossible to write about the changes Jacob Zuma must introduce without explaining the origins of the problems in the Mbeki era. In their book *Thinking in Time: The Uses of History for Decision Makers* (based on a course they co-taught at Harvard), Richard Neustadt and Ernest May explain the difficulty of separating analysis of present leaders from that of their predecessors. 'Some readers are apt to think us unduly hard on the Carter administration. We go back and back to the Carter years like someone tonguing a sensitive tooth ... The Carter presidency came and went while we were working on our course. It offered something for discussion every time the class met.' [1]

Neustadt and May wrote their book at a time when everyone, Carter's own aides included, were writing about their experiences in his administration. In these memoirs there was a sense that while not everyone agreed about what went wrong on each issue, all felt 'that what happened ought to have been preventable'. Writing as they did about the importance of history in policy-making, all agreed on another point, which has striking resonance with the Mbeki years. This was Carter's 'view of problems as technical, not historical, his lack of curiosity about how the story turned out before'.

And so in writing about South Africa's democratic moment I will from time to time allude to what Zuma has saved us from. But Zuma must also be evaluated in his own right. To a degree there is no way of avoiding the origins of problems; but to an equal degree Zuma must be held accountable for his own decisions.

In the period leading up to the April 2009 elections I used to receive invitations to address different audiences about how life would be under a Zuma administration. I usually made no more than a few points. The first was that no sooner would Zuma take office than he would be faced with throngs of former supporters demanding that he should meet their demands without delay. My favourite example was Blade Nzimande: no sooner would he be appointed minister of education than he would be faced with striking teachers demanding salary increases. I looked forward to seeing how a communist cabinet minister would respond to those demands. But Nzimande was shrewder than I thought. He chose the safe ministry of higher education: academics hardly ever go on strike. His deputy in the Communist Party, Jeremy Cronin, would not have it any easier as taxi drivers were demanding that the government abolish the new Bus Rapid Transit system. Cronin astutely pointed out that the taxi

1 Richard Neustadt and Ernest May, *Thinking in Time: Uses of History for Decision Makers* (New York: Free Press, 1986), xiv.

owners were just another self-interested business lobby. These may be shrewd manoeuvres indeed, but they point to the contradictions that face all 'left' governments: social problems do not simply disappear because a 'left' government has been elected.

During my talks I also pointed out that in addition to powerful interest groups outside their own constituencies, government leaders had to come to terms with the inertia of government bureaucracy. The transition from the fast tempo of the electoral campaign to the glacial pace of the bureaucratic machinery might be unnerving and even frustrating for the new leaders. The challenges were not only economic or political or ideological but also, ultimately, institutional. The question at the end of the day is whether the new leadership under Jacob Zuma has the emotional temperament, the ethical-moral commitment, the political willingness and the institutional resources needed to engage with communities in the resolution of those problems and the revival of democracy. If they do not, then we will be in no better position than we were under Mbcki. In fact we might even be in worse shape. In the end Mbeki's autocratic behaviour might simply be replaced by anarchy and party autocracy under Zuma. The democratic moment would have been just that – a passing moment.

Although my kids may be disappointed that this is *not* a sequel, I hope they will be satisfied that it's all for a good cause. The cause is to improve in whatever way we can the prospects for democracy in the country, for their future and that of all the children of our land. This book is inspired by the sentiments contained in the following column which I wrote in May 2008.[2]

For the first time in more than a decade I feel a sense of excitement about this country's public policy possibilities. I am sure there will be

---

2 Xolela Mangcu, 'Why living in hope is crucial as SA begins a new political era', *Business Day*, 28 May 2009.

mishaps, failures and acts of arrogance by the new government. But to live in perpetual anticipation of failure is to lead a cynical existence. The role of the critic is to live in hope.

In his book *Restoring Hope*, Cornel West argues that hope is neither optimism nor pessimism. Optimism and pessimism assume that people are spectators who survey the landscape and infer on the basis of the evidence around them that things will get better or worse. But hope assumes that people are participants who act in and on the world.

Over the past decade, we were reduced to what the Indian scholar Partha Chatterjee called 'empirical objects of government policy, not citizens who participate in the sovereignty of the state'.

But hope as activism springs eternal in South Africa, and things have changed.

So what are my hopes going into the future? Actually, they have not changed from those I expressed in the *Mail & Guardian* in 1998.

First, I suggested we should develop a national consensus – or a sense of purpose – in the full knowledge that criticism is the life blood of a democratic society.

Second, I suggested that we needed to develop community-based institutes and forums for public deliberation – in our universities, the media and, most importantly, in our communities.

Third, I said we needed to nurture the next generation of black public intellectuals. Unless we did that, there would be no one left to combat the racist stereotypes that saturate our public discourse.

Fourth, I argued that 'all of this could be one way of fostering a deliberative culture'.

Eleven years later, I am still banging this public deliberation drum, and none of my hopes have been actualised.

Fortunately, we now have a president who seems genuinely happy just being around people. I will judge him not by how much he can split hairs about public policy issues but by how much he can get all of us collectively to split hairs about those issues. He must not think for us but think with us.

He could take a lesson from former US president Ronald Reagan. Reagan did not see his job as the technical mastery of public policy – that's what ministers, bureaucrats and advisers were paid to do. Reagan, like Theodore Roosevelt long before him, saw the presidency as a 'bully pulpit' for bringing forth hope among the American people.

The great Brazilian intellectual Paolo Freire explained why he wrote a book called *Pedagogy of Hope* thus: 'We are surrounded by a pragmatic discourse that would have us adapt to the facts of reality. Dream and utopia are called not only useless, but positively impeding … It may seem strange then that I should write a book called *Pedagogy of Hope: Pedagogy of the Oppressed Revisited.*'

Freire warned that 'the attempt to do without hope in the struggle to improve the world, as if that struggle could be reduced to calculated acts alone, or a purely scientific approach, is a frivolous illusion'. All around us is evidence of the devastating consequences of that 'frivolous illusion' – from HIV/AIDS to poverty, inequality and joblessness.

It is time to make a change by adopting what Franklin D. Roosevelt called 'bold, persistent experimentation'. In doing so, we must bear in mind that governance is not a technical science in which you lock yourself in your laboratory or study and experiment on your own, deep into the night.

That's how Frankenstein's monsters are created. Governance is founded on what Steve Biko called a feedback system: 'a discussion, in other words, between those who formulate policy and those who must perceive, accept or reject policy'.

I suggest, Mr President, that you take that line and frame it next to your mirror. For as Cornel West puts it, a politically rich life 'has to do with what you see when you get up in the morning and look in the mirror and ask yourself whether you are simply wasting your time on the planet or spending it in an enriching manner'. Enriching us, as we enrich you. That should be your bargain with history, or what India's first prime minister, Jawaharlal Nehru, would have called your 'tryst with destiny'.

Use it or lose it, Mr President.

Introduction

This book explains Jacob Zuma's political accession to the presidency of South Africa as a form of cultural insurgency. I argue that the dynamic between elite and mass politics that developed around Zuma is a contemporary political expression of the old historical divide between *amaqaba* (the red people) and *amakholwa* (educated converts) in black social history. After a bruising political campaign an uneducated, traditionalist leader took over one of the most modernist movements of the twentieth century and became president of Africa's most industrialised society. This is the historical significance of the Jacob Zuma phenomenon. The reality, though, is that Zuma is a hybrid politician who cohabits the worlds of tradition and modernity in politics. To what extent will he be able to hold the two worlds together through the course of his political tenure, and what are the implications of that hybrid leadership for governance and public policy? Will Zuma ultimately become a schizophrenic leader torn between the two sides of his being, or will he, in the words of Mahatma Gandhi, build bridges between these different dimensions of our existence as a nation?

By elite politics I simply refer to the political discourse that takes place in the formal institutions of democracy: parliament, the courts, the media and the executive branch of government. By mass politics I refer to the politics of the street: what people say and do in everyday social settings. While elite political discourse tends to revolve round the principles that underpin a constitutional democracy, mass politics tends to revolve round the symbolic identifications that people create around issues such as race, class, ethnicity and marginality. As if he had South Africa in mind, Ashu Varshney argued that mass politics tends to revolve around ethnic conflicts and 'whether to forgive (or punish) the "crimes" of high state officials'. Although writing about India, Varshney captures something that has relevance for understanding mass politics around Jacob Zuma:

> whether we like such politics, it has profound consequences. In democracies, especially poor democracies, mass politics can redefine elite politics, for an accumulated expression of popular sentiments and opinions inevitably exercises a great deal of pressure on elected politicians. Elite concerns – investment tax breaks, stock market regulations, custom duties on imported cars – do not necessarily filter down to mass politics.[1]

In explaining Zuma's rise in terms of a mass–elite political dynamic I do not mean to suggest hermetically sealed social groupings that exist completely independent of each other. Elite decisions have impact on the masses on a daily basis, and the masses are not in a permanent state of revolt against the elite. The mass revolts take place within contours laid out by the rule of law and the constitution. To say Zuma did not enjoy elite support would be as absurd as suggesting that his main protagonist, Thabo Mbeki, did not enjoy mass support. Perhaps one can restate the argument by saying what the Mbeki and Zuma coalitions were not: the movement to retain Thabo Mbeki could not

1 Ashutosh Varshney, 'Mass politics or elite politics? India's economic reforms in comparative perspective', *Journal of Policy Reform*, 1 (December 1998), 301–35.

by any stretch of the imagination be said to have been led by workers and peasants, even though some of these categories of people could be found in his coalition. Similarly, the movement behind Zuma could not be said to have been powered by a sophisticated, pipe-smoking elite in elegant Armani suits, even though such types played a crucial role in giving strategic direction and funding to the coalition. By speaking about the elite and the masses I therefore simply refer to the motive forces driving the respective movements. In the chapters that follow I examine specifically how the elite employed the law and the media in trying to stave off mass support for Zuma, and how the masses showed their collective finger to the presumptive guardians of society.

$\bigcirc$

In Chapter One I argue that even though this mass revolt against elite leadership has been a rare phenomenon in the hundred-year history of the ANC, it is by no means a unique phenomenon in the world. I say 'rare' because there were revolts in the ANC's MK camps in Angola, and working-class heroes such as Josiah Gumede in the 1930s did face enormous opposition from the elite leadership of the movement. Nonetheless, in general the ANC has been led by men of letters (and they were men) who were often suspicious of the masses. In this chapter I provide the theoretical and historical background to understanding elite fear of democracy as far back as ancient Greece.

Chapter Two examines what it is that makes the elite fearful of mass political action and violent rhetoric. I do this with specific reference to the evolution of the ANC's political culture: from the polite deputations of its early leaders to the militancy of Nelson Mandela and ultimately the militarism of the Julius Malema generation. When ANC leaders complain that the ANC of Julius Malema is not their ANC, they are expressing this classically elite fear and distaste. The elite assumed (and I include myself here) that Malema's fearsome rhetoric would drive away support for the party and for Jacob Zuma. When the masses kept coming out in numbers in support of Malema and Zuma, the elite simply dismissed them as a lumpen, irrational mass. They failed to interrogate the sociological issues that underlay political support for Jacob Zuma. They forgot Frantz Fanon's historical observation that this was how the lumpen would force themselves into nationhood.

Chapter Three looks at how the criminal justice system has been used to discipline the irrational masses and their leadership. Speaking at the Platform for Public Deliberation, Vusi Pikoli, the former national director of public prosecutions, drew an analogy about law and politics that may be helpful in understanding the place of the criminal justice system in South Africa. He said that a knife in the hands of a thug can end lives while the same knife in the hands of a surgeon can save lives. Jacob Zuma's supporters argued that former president Thabo Mbeki used the criminal justice system as a knife to end Zuma's political career. Thabo Mbeki's supporters argued that Zuma would use the criminal justice system to knife their opponents and protect his friends; hence the rush to disband the elite crime-busting unit, the Scorpions. This chapter examines what are arguably the five most important judicial decisions in the history of our democracy, the Nicholson, Harms, Ngcuka, Msimang and Mpshe decisions, and the implications for our democracy of the dangerous triad of law, media and politics.

In Chapter Four I argue that the Mbeki–Zuma contest brought out the worst aspects of the media. A cursory look at the op-ed pages of the country's newspapers demonstrates how involved South Africans are in this debate. But it also demonstrates the strong anti-Zuma positions among columnists, editors and cartoonists, and how established principles such as 'innocent until proven guilty' were turned on their head in the quest to nail Zuma. And yet despite this general antipathy in the media, Zuma continued to draw tens of thousands of supporters to his gatherings in a clear demonstration of the disjuncture between elite and mass discourse, and of the irrelevance of the media in influencing mass politics.

Chapter Five is a discussion of the state of opposition politics in South Africa. Of particular interest is the emergence of the Congress of the People as the political initiative of those members of the elite who lost out against Jacob Zuma in Polokwane. But I also examine the decimation of other opposition parties by the emergence of Cope in the 2009 elections. Even though the ANC's share of the vote declined, it still remains the dominant party, even with a controversial figure like Jacob Zuma at its helm. The chapter examines the fortunes of Cope and asks whether it will portend a break from the racialised nature of South Africa's electoral politics.

Chapter Six examines Jacob Zuma's governing philosophy and style. In his speeches Zuma has promised an open and interactive government that accepts criticism and dissent. But political power has also been shown to corrupt politicians and turn them into intolerant oligarchs: in other words, having been elected by the people, they rise above the people. Will Jacob Zuma be any different from Thabo Mbeki and other African political leaders in history? How will he protect himself from falling prey to the trappings of power and intolerance? Will he be able to bring the masses with him in conversation with the elite institutions of government, and what impact might this have on governmental and political leadership in South Africa? This chapter offers us a glimpse into the kind of leader he might become.

Chapter Seven reflects on South Africa's position within the emerging world order. It suggests that South Africa and the United States could lead a new global alliance on active citizenship.

1

Elite fear of democracy: a historical perspective

Throughout history the social and economic elite have been fearful of democracy. Two thousand years ago Plato saw in democracy nothing but a recipe for disorder by people whose only virtue was that they were poor, numerous and prone to violence. He regarded the sentencing to death of Socrates as evidence of the evil of democracy. In order to restore order democrats would ultimately have to resort to the very tyranny they claimed to abhor. Plato's most famous student, Aristotle, was less dismissive of democracy. But even for him democracy stood for nothing better than naked group self-interest, which needed to be held in check by institutions specifically designed to review the opinions of the majority.

At the beginning of the modern era, Thomas Hobbes's view of democracy derived logically from his argument that men existed in a state of nature in which life was nasty, brutish and short. To Hobbes, men were just as competitive and mutually destructive in civil society as they were in the state of nature. They would always seek ways of appropriating each other's property for their own benefit. But given their equally strong desire for the good life they would also seek ways to regulate their mutually destructive instincts. They had to devise a system by which this mutual 'invasion' could be regulated through non-violent means. Hence Hobbes's idea that a self-perpetuating Leviathan – a strong state – was needed to regulate competition.

Central to Hobbes's theory of democracy was that it should be limited to those who owned property and were therefore legitimate participants in this system of mutual 'invasion'. All those who had lost their property had no claim to participate in this regime. Even the radical Levellers argued that while everyone had a right to civil liberties, those who sold their labour could not legitimately claim a right to equal participation in a political system designed specifically to regulate relations between property owners. One of the early theorists of civil society, John Locke, advanced a similar line of argument. Locke argued that even though everyone was equally entitled to property as a natural right, it was only those who had made improvements to the property who qualified for the right to it and for the right to the suffrage.

This is all by way of saying that the modern democratic era began with a system of political participation that was anti-egalitarian. Subsequent philosophers tried to extend the right to political participation to the poor. For example, the British philosopher James Mill, father of the more illustrious John Stuart Mill, was sufficiently convinced that the poor would always follow the direction of the middle classes that he saw no need for the elite to worry about extending the franchise. In fact Mill was sure that the working class posed no danger to market society. The greatest danger lay in denying them the suffrage; this was because they would 'always obtain it, either by bad means, or good. Upon this everything depends. If they obtain it by bad means, the government is bad. If they obtain it by good means, the government is sure to be good. The only good means of obtaining it are the free suffrage of the people.'[1]

---

1 James Mill, 'On the ballot', *Westminster Review*, July 1830, cited in C.B. Macpherson, *The Life and Times of Liberal Democracy* (New York: Oxford University Press, 1977), 42.

Representative democracy: the modern compromise

Representative democracy came into being as the institutional compromise necessitated by elite fear of mass rule and the growth in size of modern societies. Notwithstanding their revolutionary beginnings, both the United States and France became democracies only after the fact and as a result of much struggle. America's most influential founding father, James Madison, rejected the idea of rule by the people, as did Robespierre, one of the leaders of the French Revolution. Madison insisted that democracy must protect 'the minority of the opulent against the majority',[2] while Robespierre argued that 'democracy was not a state in which the people continuously assembled regulates by itself all public affairs'.[3]

If it was true but impractical that the people should make everyday decisions, then someone should do so on their behalf. According to Benjamin Barber, the idea of the president in the American political system was 'the crowning achievement' of the architects of representative democracy. The president would be the mediator between the people who elected him and the powerful few who actually governed the nation in the Congress. Although Barber notes the irony of a president who campaigns against the bureaucracy as if his office was independent of that very same bureaucracy, he nonetheless maintains that the creation of in-built conflict in government is the abiding genius of America's political system:

> the faith has always been that from the clash of opposites, of contraries, of extremes, of poles, will come not the victory of any one but the mediation and accommodation of them all. The American version of truth and unity, if there was to be one, could never be forged from some ideal form. It would, as Jefferson knew, have to be hammered out in the anvil of debate.[4]

2 Cited in Macpherson, *The Life and Times of Liberal Democracy*, 15n6.
3 John Dunn, *Setting the People Free: The Story of Democracy* (London: Atlantic Books, 2005), 121.
4 Benjamin Barber, *A Passion for Democracy* (Princeton, NJ: Princeton University Press, 1998), 48.

Indeed, James MacGregor Burns has described American democracy as the greatest intellectual achievement of modern times. Perhaps the greatest lasting contribution of intellectuals over the past five hundred years has been the design of differentiated institutions of government to respond to the new social differentiation, complexity and consciousness that came with the modern period. Burns lists the invention of representative government, the separation of powers between the executive, the legislature and the judiciary, as institutional manifestations of growing consciousness of individual freedom. Thus he describes the making of the American constitution as 'an explosion of political genius in 1776 … a culmination of thinking that had its sources in centuries of hard political thought and analysis'.[5] What this period and other similar periods of social and political innovation, such as the 1930s New Deal, demonstrate is that historical change is rarely, if ever, the outcome of one bold thought or action. Innovation is more often the outcome of long and hard thought that can sometimes last decades. This is something the South African elite of the Mbeki era did not understand: that an African Renaissance, for instance, could not simply be proclaimed into existence but would require long, patient institution building and cultural change.

To be sure, the exclusion of women and black people from the franchise would stand out as the greatest indictment of American and other democracies. Robert Dahl rightly notes that 'not only were large percentages of the adult male population excluded from the suffrage in most countries but until the second decade of the twentieth century only New Zealand and Australia had extended their suffrage to women in national elections'.[6] As Fareed Zakaria says, 'only in the late 1940s did most Western countries become fully fledged democracies with universal suffrage'.[7] As late in the day as

5 James MacGregor Burns, *Leadership* (New York: Harper Collins, 1978), 156.
6 Robert Dahl, *Democracy and Its Critics* (New Haven: Yale University Press, 1989), 235.
7 Fareed Zakaria, 'The rise of illiberal democracy', *Foreign Affairs*, November/December 1997, 27.

1974 'barely a quarter of the world's states met the minimal test of democracy: a place where the people are able, through universal suffrage, to choose and replace their leaders in regular, free and fair elections'.[8] Although many newly independent countries in Latin America and Africa soon replaced democratic constitutions with dictatorships, there was really no stopping the tide of democracy covered around the world. This process of democratisation that has swept the world since the 1970s has been described by Samuel Huntington as a third wave.

It took a long time indeed between James Mill's nineteenth-century injunction to extend free suffrage to everyone to the onset of the third wave in the late twentieth century. Even then democracy did not proceed in a singular form. I now turn to the two main strands of democracy and the way they have manifested themselves in South Africa. These are civic republicanism and liberal democracy.

Civic republicanism and the quest for community

While the liberal view of democracy regards the individual as existing prior to society, the republican view holds that the community is prior to the individual. Thus far I have limited the discussion of democracy to the classic liberal form which regards democracy as a system by which individual rights are secured. In this conception the individual is the centre of moral life and political life, unencumbered by social and communal pressures, particularly those of the state. But just as important in the evolution of democracy has been the civic republican strand inspired by thinkers like Jean Jacques Rousseau and Thomas Jefferson. According to this tradition individual freedom can only be secured within the context of community by means of a set of guiding values – or what Rousseau famously described as a civil religion, 'a *civil* profession of faith the articles of which it is up to the Sovereign to fix, not precisely as dogmas of Religion but as

8 Larry Diamond,'How to save democracy', *Newsweek*, 31 December 2008, 20.

sentiments of sociability, without which it is impossible to be either a good citizen or a loyal subject'.

Rousseau was not much of a democrat: according to him, the Sovereign had every right to banish those who were unsociable and 'if anyone after having publicly acknowledged these same dogmas, behaves as if he did not believe them, let him be punished with death; he has committed the greatest of crimes, he has lied before the laws'.[9] History is full of examples of how the idea of the general will that prescribes the common good can go wrong. But just as a republican politics that flouts democratic procedures can result in tyranny, a liberalism devoid of discussions of the moral good can coexist with and even justify slavery. While it is tempting to see liberalism and republicanism as ideal types, the reality is that no liberal society can survive without a modicum of values. The very principles that underpin liberalism are in and of themselves an articulation of values. Similarly, no republican regime can exist without attention to liberal procedures such as freedom of speech. Hence Alexis de Tocqueville argued forcefully that the pursuit of the general will need not be an authoritarian affair. The difference between Rousseau's autocratic republicanism and Tocqueville's democratic republicanism has been captured by Michael Sandel:

> Unlike Rousseau's unitary vision, the republican politics de Tocqueville describes is more clamorous than consensual. It does not despise differentiation. Instead of collapsing spaces between persons, it fills this space with public institutions that gather people together in various capacities, that both separate and relate them. These institutions include the towns, schools, religions, and virtue-sustaining occupations that form the 'habits of the heart' a democratic republic requires. Whatever their more particular purposes, these agencies of civic education inculcate the habit of attending to public

9 Jean Jacques Rousseau, *The Social Contract*, Book IV, Chapter 8.

things. And yet given their multiplicity, they prevent public life from dissolving into an undifferentiated whole.[10]

The beginnings of snob democracy in South Africa

Now what does all of this historical discussion have to do with South Africa's democracy? Well, to paraphrase Nathan Glazer,[11] we are all liberals now. We may be nationalists, communists or feminists but we all live under a liberal constitution at the centre of which is the protection of private property, freedom of expression, freedom of association and all the liberties that have been associated with liberal democracy. Notwithstanding the traditions of mass mobilisation and community building in the black community, the style of government that has prevailed in South Africa since 1994 has not been a departure from the elite-driven processes we have seen throughout history. In an op-ed article I wrote for the *Mail & Guardian* just before the elections that would bring Thabo Mbeki to power in 1999, I called for an end to this 'snob democracy'.[12]

The political transformation of the past 10 years will no doubt go down in history as one of the most important events of the millennium – on par with the French, American, Indian, Chinese, and Russian revolutions. Some of our leading scholars have taken to talking about the 'maturing' and 'consolidation' of our democracy, and rightly so. But self-congratulation always has to be accompanied by a willingness to talk frankly about our shortcomings as well.

There is a foundational flaw in our democracy that goes back to the early days of the transition but has become a defining characteristic of our political culture. While the political transition itself was the result

10 Michael Sandel, *Democracy's Discontent: America in Search of a Public Philosophy* (Cambridge, MA: Harvard University Press, 1996), 320–1.
11 After a lifetime writing against multiculturalism and affirmative action, the distinguished Harvard academic wrote a book titled *We Are All Multiculturalists Now* (Cambridge, MA: Harvard University Press, 1997).
12 Xolela Mangcu, 'An alternative to snob democracy', *Mail & Guardian*, 30 April 1999.

of mass mobilisation in the townships and villages of this country, the negotiations process was, at times, a secretive affair whose outcome hinged on the bargaining skills of the leaders of the various political parties, mainly the African National Congress and the National Party.

Having delegated power upwards during the negotiations, we then invested in a number of political and institutional support systems consistent with the overall emphasis on elite decision making. The centralisation of authority in national leadership; the dominant role of political parties as containers of debate, discontent and disagreement; the party list system; the concomitant emphasis on what Nelson Mandela and Thabo Mbeki would do for us; and the language of delivery are but a few manifestations of an increasingly top-down political system.

All these developments run the risk of producing a split national identity. On the one hand would be a group of political and economic elites who, by virtue of their proximate race/class distance from power, would become the real, active citizens. And on the other hand, a passive population that would be nothing more than 'empirical objects of government policy, not citizens who participate in the sovereignty of the state'.

Promises of delivery would become nothing less than 'the opiate of the masses' – the only language that the government could use to talk with its constituencies. In less than a decade we would have gone full circle from the mass clamour for democratic participation to the elite model of democracy normally associated with political snobs such as Edmund Burke and Joseph Schumpeter.

It will, of course, be argued that the negotiated transition was the only way we could have brought ourselves from the abyss of interminable racial violence. But that's only half the answer. A full answer would have to suggest how we can build on the progress of the past to deepen democratic participation in the future. As Yale University political scientist Ian Shapiro argues: 'The problem with negotiated transitions is not that the institutions are imposed from above, but rather that they are not imposed in a sufficiently thoroughgoing fashion.'

And so, for me, the most important question in the upcoming elections is not which party to vote for – since they all operate within the same elite model of democracy – but whether we can start talking about alternative models of democracy in this country. It seems to me that we need to go beyond the conception of democracy as merely the right to choose our leaders – which is a necessary but insufficient condition for democratic participation – to some kind of direct, participatory and communicative democracy.

As Steve Biko once put it: 'In a government where democracy is allowed to work, one of the principles that are normally entrenched is a feedback system, a discussion between those who formulate policy and those who must perceive, accept or reject policy. In other words, there must be a system of education, political education, and this does not necessarily go with literacy.'

Or, as Es'kia Mphahlele more recently said: 'We are wrong in thinking that because the government is democratically elected, therefore there is democracy. Democracy is about the relationship between the politicians and their constituencies, and the "African renaissance" must therefore go to the heart of the people in making them think democratically.'

Participation is the cardinal principle of democracy – not only because of its intrinsic value, but also because it increases the political efficacy of citizens by giving them direct training in the policies and tools of governance.

Almost 150 years ago, John Stuart Mill suggested that this kind of democratic training is best obtainable at the local level, where citizens can make decisions about issues they can immediately relate to, and then generalise that knowledge to the broader, national political system.

The best example of this in this country is the black consciousness movement of the 1970s. Many of our current leaders, in the public, private and non-profit sectors, received their leadership training through the political education and development programmes of organisations such as the Black Community Programmes – even if some of them would now disavow black consciousness politics. But, even if people do not agree with the substance of black consciousness, we can at least go back to the veritable tradition of conscientisation that was the hallmark and signal achievement of that movement.

As the development economist Albert Hirschman has observed, the social energies that are aroused in the course of a social movement do not disappear when that movement does, but are kept in storage and become available to fuel later and sometimes different social movements.

Or, as Ashu Varshney puts it: 'While futures are indeed created, they are not typically created on a clean slate. It is hard for nations to leave their pasts behind. The more pertinent issue is: how does a nation reconstruct its past? Which traditions should be revived, and which ones dropped? The ideological task is to retrieve that which is valuable, and to make this selective retrieval a political reality.'

There are a number of reasons why governments tend to remain snobbish. I have already alluded to the antecedents of elite fear of democracy in history. But there are also the centripetal tendencies that Robert Michels called 'the iron law of oligarchy'. This is because 'having been elected by the people, leaders inexorably rise above the people', either to protect their own self-interest or because they get so absorbed with the workings of government that they forget that another world exists on the other side of the tracks. To be sure, in the recent South African context this is not to say that the new elite did not attempt to offer a more progressive civil religion. But the elitism worsened under the leadership of President Thabo Mbeki. Let us take two examples: reconciliation and development.

Individual over communal reconciliation

Nelson Mandela will go down in history as the father of our nation, the man who brought us back from the precipice of racial conflict. His actions in this regard are well documented, and so are those of the chairman of the Truth and Reconciliation Commission, Desmond Tutu. These achievements notwithstanding, South Africa still remains a racially polarised society. The spatial geography of apartheid remains intact and the black section of society remains disproportionately poor and marginalised from the mainstream of the economy. Part of the problem is that reconciliation was limited to the perpetrators and victims of apartheid repression, that is the individual actors on the stage of the drama of struggle. Very little was done to take the processes of reconciliation into communities.

This is partly why Mandela's reconciliatory gestures to the white community came to be viewed with increasing suspicion in the black community. In the final analysis reconciliation degenerated into a 'live and let live' philosophy of mutual coexistence. The South African political discourse is classically liberal with an emphasis on the protection of property rights, freedom of speech and so on. In the liberal framework different segments of the community can remain antagonistic towards each other because nothing draws them out of their cocoons to embrace each other as members of a single community, as long as they are all protected from each other by the slate of rights in the constitution. Communities can exist in some kind of 'cold war' with each other. Benign neglect becomes part of the public culture, and service delivery a palliative for underlying inequalities. Michael Sandel describes the operation of this public philosophy as follows: 'rather than promote a particular conception of the good life, liberal political theory insists on toleration, fair procedures, and respect for individual rights – values that respect people's freedom to choose their own values.'[13]

13 Michael Sandel, *Democracy's Discontent*, 7–8.

Under Thabo Mbeki's administration, Mandela's conception of reconciliation as forgiveness was replaced by a radically different interpretation of reconciliation as transformation. But even ostensibly radical ideas such as the African Renaissance have done very little to bring about this sense of connectedness to community. The idea of the African Renaissance barely travelled beyond the circles of its chief architect, Thabo Mbeki. Instead of being a community-deep and community-wide vehicle of social engagement, the African Renaissance was reduced to no more than a couple of conferences in the plush neighbourhoods of Johannesburg. A few publications came out of the conferences but overall the African Renaissance amounted to no more than the consolidation of elite networks both within South Africa and between South Africans and the rest of the continent. As a result the black elite in South Africa are no more connected to the communities from which they come than their white counterparts. The black nationalist leadership appropriated concepts such as *ubuntu* to appeal for a new solidarity, but something seemed to hold them back from getting out into the communities to make the connections that would bring *ubuntu* forth.

Interestingly, the most republican of all of our liberation movements was in some ways the black consciousness movement, with its emphasis on community building through social solidarity. Through the Black Community Programmes the movement sponsored development initiatives throughout the country in the 1970s, from building schools and clinics to starting newspapers and research institutions. The idea was not only to employ black people but to provide a sense of ownership that would give people enough of a stake in the projects that they would be prepared to protect their livelihoods through political action. The movement also sought to create a society in which community came first. At the heart of the movement was a critique of Western liberal individualism, the very liberal individualism that would come to define black social culture in the post-democratic era. Steve Biko's critique of Western liberal individualism went as follows:

> In rejecting Western values, therefore, we are rejecting only those things that are not only foreign to us but seek to destroy the most cherished of our beliefs – that the corner-stone of society is man himself – not just his welfare, not his material well-being but just man himself with all his ramifications ... we believe that in the long run the special contribution to the world by Africa will be in this field of human relationships. The great powers of the world may have done wonders in giving the world an industrial and military outlook, but the great gift still has to come from Africa – giving the world a more human face.[14]

The rise of struggle and decline of community in the 1980s

The black consciousness movement was destroyed when all the organisations associated with it were banned in the late 1970s and their assets confiscated by the state. The greatest blow was the death of its leader, Steve Biko. Into the void entered a new political tradition that led to a disconnection with community. There is no question that the political activism of the 1980s was both more militant and militaristic than that of the black consciousness era. The organisation building of the 1970s was replaced by a dizzying pace of mass mobilisation. When the young lions of the 1980s took to heart Oliver Tambo's call to make the country 'ungovernable', this led to the destruction of apartheid authority structures such as the dummy local authorities that existed in the townships.

Unfortunately, the violence also turned inward. The dreaded and dreadful necklace – a burning tyre placed around a victim's neck – was used to eliminate suspected spies. Activists also imposed consumer boycotts as a weapon of struggle against local authorities, but their

14 Steve Biko, *I Write What I Like* (Johannesburg: Picador, 2004), 51.

enforcement also meant that those who violated or were in breach of the boycott became victims of violence, often meted out by youth to adults old enough to be their parents. Lastly, the credo of 'liberation before education' would have long-term negative effects as young black militants abandoned schooling for the thrill of activism. The late editor of the *Sowetan*, Aggrey Klaaste, described the 1980s as the period in which 'blacks lost many things. Worst of all we lost the innocence of our children. We also lost their respect for us.' Klaaste observed:

> the scars of 1976 were on the way to being healed when the next conflagration struck with phenomenal intensity. This was September 1984 … it took the security forces and the police a longish time to deal with the violence unleashed in 1984 and onwards. They looked on with sadistic fascination as the black community was seemingly engaged in tearing itself apart.[15]

Some of that 'insanity' played out in the grass-covered and rolling hills of KwaZulu-Natal. Thousands of people lost their lives in the killing fields of this province but the violence spread beyond to Gauteng. The apartheid police played their part in spurring on the conflict through the actions of the so-called Third Force. There was also the violent conflict between ANC supporters in the civic movements and the United Democratic Front, on the one hand, and the Azanian People's Organisation, on the other. In short the 1980s were a bloody affair.

It is of course important to locate the growing violence not only within the context of the intensifying struggle by the ANC and mass democratic movement but also within the context of growing joblessness in the townships. The 1970s was a time of economic

15 Aggrey Klaaste, 'The thinking behind nation building' in J. Wentzel, *The Liberal Slideaway* (Johannesburg, 1995).

contraction in South Africa. Coming after what has sometimes been described as the golden age, the economy shrank in the mid-1970s because of both a decline in the terms of trade for South Africa's exports and a decline in investment in manufacturing. Faced with decreasing prospects of earning any livelihood in the homelands, increasing numbers of people moved to the cities in large numbers at a time when the cities struggled to absorb them into any form of productive employment.[16] The cities were not just a centre of heightened political mobilisation but also an economic time-bomb waiting to explode. And explode they did with frightening intensity.

From self-reliant development to service delivery

Into the void left by the demise of black consciousness emerged what I have described as 'technocratic creep' in public policy discussions. After nearly a decade of civic mobilisation in the 1980s, academic experts from some of the country's leading universities and think-tanks started providing technical assistance to the civic organisations that were taking control of the townships. Despite their power to mobilise communities, the civic organisations were mostly ignorant about public policy. In a dramatic departure from black consciousness practices, they relied on white consultants for advice. Black cultural agency and self-reliance was replaced by a non-racial modernism. This reversal of roles – with white policy experts taking over leadership and black political leaders following their cues – took place in the negotiating forums that emerged in the late 1980s to replace apartheid local government structures. These forums were extended to the national level through bodies such as the National Housing Forum (NHF). One of the participants in the NHF describes how the technocrats took over the public policy function:

16 Dan O'Meara, *Forty Lost Years* (Johannesburg: Ravan Press, 1996).

many of the representatives, while not necessarily experts in the housing field, brought other valuable skills and experience to the process. The civic and mass-based organizations brought a strong constituency base and the promise of a widely consulted mandate for the development of housing policy, as well as in-depth experience in grassroots conditions, expectations and needs. Business organizations brought an understanding of the *technical* detail of the housing sector and of the possibilities for growth and development within it. The business sector also had *practical* experience: many had burnt fingers and others had pulled out of the low-income housing market entirely. The development organizations brought development expertise and an understanding of the interaction between policy and practice.[17]

In short, while business and policy institutions brought technical expertise, the role of civil society groups was to take care of the softer issues of community participation. Further insight into the dynamics within the NHF is provided by these comments:

People who were committed to the symbolic side of the process featured very strongly before the founding of the NHF. The initial players were highly skilled in bringing the right people together around a common theme and holding them there as a symbolic gesture of unity. Once this aspect of the process was over, the technocrats who had a capacity for process issues as well, featured much more strongly.[18]

This was also a reflection of the fact that the ANC had no housing policy to speak of when it was unbanned and its leaders returned

17 Matthew Nell, Ishmael Mkhabela, Kecia Rust and Piet du Plessis, 'Strategy and tactics: planning and management in the NHF' in Kecia Rust and Sue Bernstein (eds.), *A Mandate to Build: Developing a Consensus around a National Housing Policy in South Africa* (Johannesburg: Ravan Press, 1996), 40.
18 Ibid., 59.

from exile, nor did the civic movements. As it turned out, the people who played a central role in forums like the NHF joined the first democratic government as directors-general and policy-makers. Thus began the process of rule by experts that has come to characterise South Africa's approach to development.

But this technocratic approach, which was adopted by the Mandela government, was also consistent with the liberal elite culture of the Mbeki era. Mbeki saw himself as a liberal aristocrat who could not be bothered with the mob. Instead of the masses being seen as potential agents of development, they were reduced to the role of consumers of development. Service delivery replaced the ideas of community self-reliance and identity which had performed such a useful role in different stages of the liberation struggle, particularly in the 1970s. South Africa's official conceptions of development are consistent with the liberal consumer conception of democracy described by the political thinker C.B. Macpherson:

> In this model there is no enthusiasm for democracy, no idea that it could be a morally transformative force … its advocacy is based on the assumption that man is an infinite consumer, that his overriding motivation is to maximize the flow of satisfactions or utilities to himself from society, and that a national society is simply a collection of such individuals.[19]

Conclusion: the new challenge to the left

The evolution of South Africa's democracy has been no different from that of democracy elsewhere in history. Not only is it dressed up in liberal clothing but it has been characterised by elite fear of the masses, elite-driven reconciliation processes and the concomitant consumerist conception of development. Elites have argued that the South African economy can no longer be expected to create jobs and

19 C.B. Macpherson, *The Life and Times of Liberal Democracy*, 43.

that even the idea of people working throughout the year is a luxury. With growing unemployment the government has turned to social grants to ameliorate social suffering. Thirteen million South Africans – eight million of them children – exist on the social grant system.

This welfarisation of society makes age-old concepts such as the working class far less useful in explaining the social forces behind the rise of Jacob Zuma. Rather we should see these new social and political actors as constituting what Ernesto Laclau calls the 'underdogs'. They have their own culture, language and styles of mobilisation. With a background similar to many of them, Jacob Zuma has become their hero: the classic populist, anti-establishment figure. Since his rise to power, the old elite has often looked askance and asked with a mix of incredulity and self-righteousness, 'What happened to our movement? What happened to our country?' Well, what happened was that the great unwashed took over the centre stage of the evolving political drama.

But this is not just a challenge to liberal elites. Even the trade unions, that classic modernist creation of the British working classes, cannot speak for 'these people'. Laclau and Mouffe argue that there is no longer any need to give primacy to the working class as the motive force of history. The emergence of new social movements organised around issues of race, gender, environment and so on has meant that it is not one's relation to the means of production that determines one's social consciousness. Laclau and Mouffe argue that if it is to operate on a mass terrain, then the working class has to recompose itself in alliance with other political groupings: 'it must abandon its class ghetto and transform itself into the articulator of a multiplicity of antagonisms and demands stretching beyond itself'.[20] Laclau and Mouffe were no doubt influenced by Antonio Gramsci's idea that social unity must be predicated on the acknowledgement

20 Ernest Laclau and Chantal Mouffe, *Hegemony and Socialist Strategy* (London: Verso, 1986), 58.

of the heterogeneity and plurality of society. Laclau has returned to this subject of heterogeneity in his new, aptly titled book, *On Populist Reason*: 'any kind of underdog … has to have something of the nature of a lumpenproletariat if it is going to be an antagonistic subject'.[21]

Many of Zuma's supporters constitute what Marx would dismiss as the lumpenproletariat with no historical consciousness. Indeed, even some analysts in South Africa have dismissed the people who support Zuma in similar terms. Achille Mbembe has likened them to a millenarian movement. But Frantz Fanon had an appreciation for the political agency of this social stratum, as did Steve Biko. What is not clear is whether the new ANC, including the leftists within it, ever had this appreciation beyond the time of elections. Did they ever sit down to think about what it would take to govern with the lumpenproletariat? Does any social movement ever stop to think of the challenges of incorporating the masses into its philosophy of rule?

In the next chapter I shall discuss the impact of the culture of the 'underdog' on the ANC's political culture and on the country more broadly. Suffice it to say that having been elected in the face of an elite liberal opposition and having ridden the wave of mass popular discontent, Jacob Zuma now stands poised between the liberal elite culture of 'live and let live' and the militaristic, radical lumpen culture of 'gimme, gimme, gimme'. Notwithstanding differences in their class origins, the elite and the lumpen share something in common: a consumerist conception of democracy and development. The question is whether Jacob Zuma can do anything to turn that culture around and revive the best traditions of black civic life based on community building and self-reliant development. Let us now examine the nature of the beast of militarism in the early days of the Zuma campaign.

---

21 Ernesto Laclau, *On Populist Reason* (London: Verso, 2005), 152.

2

'We will kill for Zuma': militarism as the new politics of authenticity

The new political culture

For the most part political philosophers have defined political culture as the set of attitudes and sentiments that underpin a political system. Drawing on the work of James Coleman, Lucian Pye described political culture as 'the set of attitudes, beliefs, and sentiments which give order and meaning to a political process and which provide the underlying assumptions and rules that govern behavior in the political system'. Sydney Verba defined political culture as a system of control vis-à-vis the system of political interactions'.[1] Robert Dahl argues that 'taken together, beliefs, attitudes, and predispositions form a political culture, or perhaps several political subcultures into which activists and citizens are socialized in varying degrees'.[2] According to these descriptions any political system depends for its proper functioning on that society's political culture in the same way that a motor car needs its engine to be oiled. Or as C.B. Macpherson put it: 'the workability of any political system depends largely on how all the other institutions,

1 Pye and Verba cited in Jeremy Gould, 'Conceptualizing political culture', Paper given at the Interrogating the New Political Culture in Southern Africa Conference, Harare, 13–15 June 2001.
2 Robert Dahl, *Democracy and Its Critics* (New Haven: Yale University Press, 1989), 262.

social and economic, have shaped, or might shape, the people with whom the political system must operate'.[3] At the heart of the concept of political culture is the related concept of political authority. In other words, how receptive are people to social and political regulation by the ruling elite? What are their attitudes towards institutions of authority and authority figures?

John Dunn makes a similar point about the role of overarching values or what he calls conceptions. He argues that even though modern institutions are vastly different from those of Athens two thousand years ago, what connects us to the ancients are certain normative conceptions:

> conceptions of this kind (values, ideals, visions of life) never determine the outcome of the politics of any community, and change constantly as they shape and reshape purposes along the way. But no community can exist even fugitively, let alone persist and extend across long spans of time, except by courtesy of just such conceptions, and the complicated tissue of institutions and practices which they inform and sustain.[4]

The problem with much discussion of political culture or 'conceptions', or what Max Weber called 'legitimations', is that such discussions often proceed as if the making of value orientations takes place in a vacuum. In the words of C. Wright Mills, such discussions tend to transform 'all institutional structures into a moral sphere'. Citizens have to get along or face being described as deviant without any examination of the structural foundations of their behaviour (hence the easy tendency to describe Zuma's followers as deviants). And yet these conceptions of what constitutes political normality and morality are a site of endless contestation:

3 C.B. Macpherson, *The Life and Times of Liberal Democracy* (New York: Oxford University Press, 1977)..

4 John Dunn, *Setting the People Free* (London: Atlantic Books, 2005), 31.

we may not yet assume that some such set of values, or legitimations, must prevail lest a social structure come apart, nor may we assume that a social structure must be made coherent or unified by any such 'normative structure'. Certainly we may not merely assume that any such normative structure as may prevail is, in any meaning of the word, autonomous ... often there are quite well-organized symbols of opposition which are used to justify insurgent movements and to debunk ruling authorities.[5]

Historical contestations of political culture in South Africa

As I argued in the last chapter, democratic participation was historically the preserve of a small elite until that conception came under attack through successive insurgent social movements. South African history has been characterised by this contest with political authority over the conceptions or values that should inform our political system. The struggle has taken on different forms. Black people first resisted colonial encroachment and the imposition of colonial rule in the Cape by force of arms. After a hundred years' war on the plains and mountains of the Eastern Cape – the so-called frontier wars – the resistance moved to KwaZulu-Natal and other parts of the country.

Facing defeat, black people sought and found ways of integrating into the 'onrush of modernity' that came with the imposition of colonial and missionary authority.[6] It was a violent modernity that held Europe to be the apex of human civilisation and ultimately spawned the Verwoerdian pipedream of a society in which whites and blacks would live apart, with blacks existing only to minister with the needs of whites. Blacks responded by patiently pleading with whites to grant them, or at least some of them, political rights. As with the

5 C. Wright Mills, *The Sociological Imagination* (New York: Oxford University Press, 1959), 25–49.
6 Eric Hobsbawm, *Nations and Nationalism since 1780* (Cambridge: Cambridge University Press, 1990), 109.

history of democracy in general, those with education and property sought a place only for themselves at the table.

In the 1940s this conservative, patrician leadership was openly challenged and replaced by a militant nationalism that did not want only inclusion in the political system but full equality. When that did not happen, the militants – now in alliance with communists – abandoned their non-violent protests to take up arms for their freedom. With the rise of the black consciousness movement, the Pan Africanist Congress and later the ANC's People's War, the language was no longer that of inclusion in the political system. Black people wanted not only to be included but to be the pace-setters of their own freedom. If the black consciousness movement sought to dislodge the association of whiteness with authority through mental liberation, the ANC's People's War sought to dislodge white authority physically from the seat of power through four strategies: an extensive underground network; mass political action; armed struggle; and an international campaign to isolate the apartheid regime from the rest of the world community. The campaign led ultimately to the historic political compromise that ushered in democracy in 1994 under the skilful leadership of Nelson Mandela and F.W. de Klerk.

Since then South Africa has had a double transition. The first transition was relatively straightforward – if not in practice, then at least in its intention and rationale. Black people, who had been victims of colonial takeover and formed by far the majority of the population, had to take over the rule of the country. This they did with aplomb, leading many to describe the transition as a miracle, the seventh wonder of the world. And the politics of the first decade of democracy proceeded rather predictably. Some years ago when I hosted a panel discussion at the University of Cape Town for a group of Rockefeller Foundation Fellows, one of the speakers captured this dynamic by saying that 1994 meant two different things for blacks and whites. For blacks it was the beginning of freedom and for whites it represented the end of freedom. It followed then that blacks and whites would approach political authority differently. Blacks were generally supportive of the leadership of Nelson Mandela to the extent of not wanting to criticise him in any way. He was the saint of our politics – although I did venture to point out some of my differences with him. I was not particularly enamoured of his constant reassurance of white people without addressing the psychological, let alone economic, needs of the black majority. But he remained our patron saint nonetheless.

Mark Gevisser has described the South African transition as consisting of three stages: from Mandela to Thabo Mbeki to Jacob Zuma. I see it differently. Mandela and Mbeki may not have had much in common in terms of their political temperament: Mandela was known for his inclusive politics while Mbeki's basic instinct was to exclude and banish. But on the whole they were both part of the long line of missionary-educated graduates who had led the ANC since its founding almost a century ago. Over the hundred or so years of its existence the ANC was always led by the schooled people: doctors, lawyers, priests and economists such as Thabo Mbeki.

The second transition proper began when Jacob Zuma took over the ANC, shaking the very foundations of the taken-for-granted assumption that the educated shall lead. He is the first leader of the ANC never to have seen the inside of a classroom. He was the self-taught child of a domestic worker and a father whom he never knew. In *The Dream Deferred*, Mark Gevisser outlined Mbeki's rather privileged and alienated existence in his rural village of Idutywa. His early life was spent reading letters to the unlettered people of Idutywa. Change a few facts such as place of birth, and Jacob Zuma could easily have been one of those people listening attentively to the words falling from young Mbeki's lips. And now here was Zuma committing the great sin of challenging his 'teacher', against the best traditions of his movement. Not only that, but this uneducated man also wanted to take over the running of the most powerful country on the African continent.

The idea that the ANC could be led by an unschooled individual was a culture shock in another sense. The rebellion against Thabo Mbeki at the ANC's Polokwane conference in 2007 represented a challenge not just to the elite prerogative to lead but also to the decorum of political deliberation. There is something unsettling to the elite sensibility about the loudness of the mob. One saw it in Thabo Mbeki's face as the crowd at Polokwane booed and jeered him. He might have easily said what Nehru is reported to have asked Gandhi at a mass rally in India: 'What do I have in common with these people?' The chairman of the ANC, Mosiuoa Lekota, tried to restore order but the crowd would have none of it. It took the party's secretary-general, Kgalema Motlanthe, to walk on to the stage to calm the crowd.

One of the starkest challenges to elite prerogative came with the dispute about the counting process in the election of the new ANC leader. Jacob Zuma's supporters insisted on manual counting because they feared that the electronic system had been rigged by Mbeki's people. This tussle between manual labour and technology stood as a metaphor signifying the difference between the anti-modern and the modern, except that the modern had lost all authority. The anti-modern had their way not only with the method but with the outcome of the meeting. I exaggerate of course. Zuma's team consisted of some of the most sophisticated, modern players in the ANC. But there could be no question that on the whole a different cast of characters was about to take over.

Even though Zuma was not my ideal candidate for the leadership of the ANC, and by extension of the country, I was pleased that Mbeki had been ousted at Polokwane. The reasons for that are laid out in my previous book, *To the Brink*. Suffice it to say that the man had become an autocrat whose racialised views on HIV/AIDS,

Zimbabwe, crime and corruption had done everything to undermine our democracy. I would venture to say that without Mbeki there would have been no Jacob Zuma or Julius Malema. That's what it had to take to get rid of him. According to Achille Mbembe, Mbeki 'made enemies of people who could have been his friends and of those he could have easily won over by charm, persuasion, or simply by carefully listening to them'. Mbembe says Mbeki made these enemies because 'he never really achieved the kind of inner peace and inner joy that could have set him on the path towards authentic freedom – freedom from past wounds, pettiness, paranoia, vindictiveness and lack of generosity'.[7]

I celebrated the news of Mbeki's defeat with my friends in my township.[8]

If you ask me, I'd rather still be in bed recovering from the holidays. A holiday is rather a misnomer when I go home. I spent the holidays partying, hanging out at the beach, playing golf, drinking at my friend Viwe's shebeen in Ginsberg. I went around Eastern Cape with my other buddy, Ben Jonas, winning golf tournaments. To be sure, he did the winning and I did most of the enjoyment. One of the prizes we won was a whole lot of meat at the King William's Town Golf Club.

He's still sulking and not talking to me because I braaied and ate the meat with other friends without his knowledge. Sweet revenge, I say. The guy had been helping himself to my whisky without my knowledge and now he's crying.

And that's the same guy who sent me a message saying: 'Best wishes for the new year to you and JZ.' He was not the only one to accuse me so. About half a dozen people made the same accusation. Someone would walk into the shebeen, buy a beer, sit quietly for a

7 Achille Mbembe, 'When the dust settles, SA will note his good work', *The Star*, 1 October 2008.
8 Xolela Mangcu, 'Ngcu boy, you guys must be celebrating', *The Weekender*, 12–13 January 2008.

while, and then say: 'Ah, Ngcu-boy, you guys must be celebrating; your man has won.' I simply refused to be drawn into any political discussion.

But after a few helpings of good Scotch, the inhibitions went away and I was all agog about how great it was that the country was now relieved of Mbeki.

Someone sent me the following SMS: 'Free at last, ma Jola. That's the country you return to post-Polokwane. A victory you helped usher in with your pen and prose. You helped demystify the age of arrogance and intellectual thuggery. We have a reason to celebrate. Freedom from denialism, delusion and intellectual pretensions. Happy holidays.' I try to explain to my buddies that I would have preferred Tokyo Sexwale or anybody else other than Mbeki or Zuma. In the final analysis, I came to support Zuma as Mbeki was the greater danger to our society.

So much for trying to be nuanced at 1 am after a good helping of Scotch, music blaring in the background and everyone hollering at you. There's no Dr Mangcu here. It's Ngcu-boy arguing endlessly with his childhood friends.

I should also say that some of these dudes have had varied experiences with the law, to put it mildly. Some of them have been on the wrong side of the law for so long that they have pretty intimate knowledge of the functioning of the criminal justice system. I'm afraid what they have to say will come as cold comfort to JZ. They asked me to take with me a message to my 'friend JZ'. In their respective experiences, it is unheard of for anyone to escape 18 charges. And so they tell me that JZ may have won the battle but will certainly lose the war for the South African presidency.

By opposing Mbeki's attempt to get a third term, I was automatically Zuma's man, my nuanced argument for a third candidate notwithstanding. The beauty of all of this is that these buddies of mine are Mbeki-ites and we can break bread together. There's a lesson there for both Mbeki-ites and Zuma-ites in the ANC. Kiss and make up, which is exactly what I have to do with the friend whose meat I ate. Hard but necessary.

The nation's eyes were now focused on the new leadership headed by Jacob Zuma. How would they acquit themselves in power? Would they open up the political culture? Some of the early decisions of the new leadership were encouraging in their level-headedness. For example, the party's new parliamentary subcommittee heads consisted of a mix of youth and experience: from Fikile Mbalula heading up the political campaigns subcommittee to Pallo Jordan heading up the communications subcommittee. Other subcommittee heads included well-known and respected figures such as Max Sisulu (economic transformation); Ebrahim Ebrahim (international relations), Siphiwe Nyanda (defence), Lindiwe Sisulu (social transformation), and Zola Skweyiya and Cyril Ramaphosa.

The revival of militarism
The excitement of a well-managed transition was, however, short-lived. The level-headedness was soon followed by an almost inexplicable irascibility coming out of the party headquarters in Luthuli House. Party secretary-general Gwede Mantashe fired the first salvo by attacking the deputy chief justice of the Constitutional Court, Dikgang Moseneke, for remarks he had made at a private function. Moseneke was reported to have said that he would not take orders from the ANC. Mantashe described the Constitutional Court justices as counter-revolutionaries bent on reversing the gains that had been made since 1994. It was a shocking statement because on the face of it there was nothing wrong in what Moseneke had said. The problem is that he said it at a private party attended by some of Thabo Mbeki's staunchest defenders, including the notorious former national director of public prosecutions, Bulelani Ngcuka, the man Mbeki is alleged to have used to persecute Zuma.

Hot on the heels of Mantashe's statement, the ANC's treasurer-general, Mathews Phosa, gave party members an ultimatum. They would have to toe the party line coming from Luthuli House or risk 'redeployment'. Phosa's eyes were set firmly on those provincial premiers seen to be closely aligned to Mbeki. And indeed the first to go were Eastern Cape premier Nosimo Balindlela and Ebrahim Rasool in the Western Cape. Balindlela complained that she first heard of her redeployment while on a trip to China, while Rasool was lucky enough to be given an advisory position in President Kgalema Motlanthe's office – an indication of ANC sensitivity to Rasool's supporters in the Western Cape.

While Phosa was issuing these ultimatums to party members, he also invited the public to participate in ANC discussions. It did not strike him that there was something odd about this invitation – that he wanted the public to come to the party as opposed to the party reaching out to the public. But this was consistent with the growing view within the ANC that the party was the centre of power – forgetting that the constitution was the source of all power. It looked as if there would be no fundamental break or difference with the Mbeki model. While Mbeki sought loyalty to his person, the new leadership sought loyalty to the party. The iron law of oligarchy that had gripped the party under Mbeki was showing itself just as menacingly under his successors. And so while my first article for *The Weekender* had been a moment of celebration of Mbeki's ousting, my first column for *Business Day* only a few weeks later was a lament about how much things promised to stay the same.[9]

I start my first column of the year with a wager. I suggest that you cut it out, file it away, and pull it out five years down the line. The wager is simple: the incoming crop of ANC leaders are likely to behave in ways that are not radically different from their predecessors.

9 Xolela Mangcu, ' The ANC and the iron law of oligarchy', *Business Day*, 24 January 2008.

While the reassertion of the political party is in some ways a good thing for democracy, one of the most enduring observations about political parties is the one articulated by Robert Michels in his study of German political parties almost 100 years ago. This is the idea that political parties tend towards the 'iron law of oligarchy'. They tend to be centralised, insular, defensive and intolerant, whoever the incumbents are.

Sociologist Alvin Gouldner described this organisational condition as 'metaphysical pathos'. However, Gouldner was also quick to suggest that political agency within organisations can lead to their democratisation. This is what we saw with the rebellion against Thabo Mbeki. Other scholars have suggested that we need to look far beyond political parties for our democracies to survive. Whether oligarchy or democracy will prevail in the new ANC is anyone's guess.

My own sense is that there is no getting around the oligarchy. There can be no greater illustration of this than the ANC leadership's most recent behaviour. Jacob Zuma's depiction of the media as an enemy is unfortunate, counterproductive and ultimately futile. The ANC can set up a media tribunal if it likes but it will soon find, like so many authoritarian governments have found out before, that you cannot control what people say or write without running into enforcement difficulties and without inviting international opprobrium. The challenge of leadership is not so much to set yourself up against the media as it is to leverage the media in all of its complexity to share your vision, solicit ideas, and generate public debates about public policy. Any leader worth his or her name will use the media to tap into the collective genius of a society.

But then, political parties would rather create nonexistent enemies so they can keep themselves internally mobilised and their leaders internally buffered. But they should be warned that political power is not the same thing as social and cultural power. The new leaders in the ANC may have won the battle against their political rivals in the ANC but they will lose in the bigger war for social and cultural power in society if they behave like bullies. Mbeki tried his hand at bullying through intellectual pretence, and the present group are trying it through militarism. Take as yet another example the reaction to Dikgang Moseneke, a well-respected jurist. While the attack on Moseneke may have been a display of political brawn and militarism, it dissipates the ANC's social and cultural power. And if ANC deputy president Kgalema Motlanthe is going to spend his precious time running around putting out fires started by his own comrades, then he is going to be burnt out before he realises it.

And then the splits will happen. They will happen also for reasons that have to do with the operation of populist movements. As Ernesto Laclau argues in *On Populist Reason*, the different factions that provided the populist frontier begin to vie for their individual and factional interests. The trouble is that there are never enough positions and there is never enough patronage to go around. There is no reason why the populist coalition should not come under similar strains.

By the way, there is an interesting entry on populism in Wikipedia. It should come in handy in discussions of populism as a political category and not a venting of prejudice against political opponents. Anyway, my point is it cannot be that the ANC's raison d'être at this historical juncture is simply that of protecting one individual. After all, the ANC is voted into power by millions of people so it can implement its electoral promises. The individualisation of the movement around Zuma is likely to be no different from the individualisation of the party under Mbeki, with ghastly consequences for society as a whole.

In my recently published book, *To the Brink: The State of Democracy in South Africa*, I argue that future generations will look back on the present crop of leaders as transitional. They performed an important role in getting rid of a would-be dictator but when their turn came they were found to be not any different. In short, tread carefully, comrades, and beware of the triumphalism that comes with newness.

The spectre of violence

If racial nativism was the badge of authenticity under Mbeki, militarism threatened to be the new badge of authenticity under Zuma. By militarism I refer to much more than the threat of violence as a way of resolving political differences. I also mean an intolerant political culture rooted in the authoritarian military tradition of the ANC underground. Armies, after all, are not particularly democratic institutions.

According to the ANC veteran Raymond Suttner, the curtailment of democracy in the ANC underground was necessitated by the vicissitudes of existence under constant enemy surveillance, and the extent of democratic debate depended on the prevailing conditions. For the most part the authoritarian culture that came to infect the ANC seeped in through the policy of democratic centralism, which required that after democratic deliberation the minority view should be subordinate to that of the majority. Suttner argues that secretiveness, conspiratorial thinking and brutality were necessary at the time to protect the party from infiltration and to operate effectively underground. These qualities, which are so essential to underground existence, 'ran counter to the normal practices of open, democratic political activity – but of course, they were dictated by unusual circumstances'.[10] According to Suttner, 'the notion of underground, the space where dangerous, heroic acts occur, signified an invisible area, a zone outside the vision of society'.[11] It is in terms of this experience that the ANC's secretive, conspiratorial thinking of recent years has been explained. The extent to which it sees itself as existing outside the purview of society has led some of its members to believe they can get away with corrupt activities. There is also a very real sense that the revolution may still be undermined.

In *Comrades against Apartheid*, Stephen Ellis and Tsepo Sechaba

10 Raymond Suttner, *The ANC Underground in South Africa to 1976: A Social and Historical Study* (Johannesburg: Jacana, 2008), 88.
11 Ibid., 93.

(Oyama Mabandla)[12] provide a rich history of communist 'entryism' in the ANC. In their version the South African Communist Party (SACP) achieved this by occupying influential roles within the ANC. The ANC's military wing, Umkhonto weSizwe (MK), came directly under the strategic direction and discipline of the Party through the critical leadership roles played by Joe Slovo and Chris Hani. Chris Hani was both political commissar of MK, which meant second-in-command of the military, and a member of the SACP's Politburo. Joe Slovo was also at one point chief of staff of MK and therefore third-in-command and a member of the Politburo. In 1987 he resigned from his position as chief of staff of MK to take up the position of general secretary of the SACP. Slovo was succeeded as chief of staff by Chris Hani, who was then ANC political commissar. Why would Hani demote himself from second-in-command to third-in-command? Well, he did not have to. All that such a powerful man needed to do was convince his comrades that the position of chief of staff needed to be upgraded to second-in-command in line with the practice of the Communist Party of the Soviet Union. The position of political commissar was thus demoted to third in seniority. It was generally expected that Siphiwe Nyanda, a non-communist military leader, would replace Hani as political commissar. However, Hani outmanoeuvred Nyanda and succeeded in getting a member of the SACP, Steve Tshwete, to take over as political commissar.

Central to the Party's control and discipline of ANC cadres was the notorious security unit known as Mbokodo. Under the pretext of sniffing out potential spies, Mbokodo punished dissenting voices by locking them up at Quatro camp (so named after the Fort, 'Number Four' jail in Johannesburg) in Angola. The reach of Mbokodo was such that even a senior leader of the ANC like Pallo Jordan was once held there for several months. Mbokodo's activities led to a mutiny

12 Stephen Ellis and Tshepo Sechaba, *Comrades Against Apartheid* (London: James Currey, 1992).

within the army ranks, which was brutally put down by Hani on the instruction of ANC military headquarters in Angola. Suttner agrees that the influence of the SACP was disproportionate to its membership in the ANC but he is less willing to go as far as Ellis and Mabandla in arguing for communist control of the ANC.

The ANC-SACP underground work was but one part of the mix in the ANC's strategy of People's War in the 1980s. The other was direct mass action to make the country ungovernable. This movement built on the civic mobilisation that had begun earlier in the decade. As pointed out in Chapter One, while the mass action quickened the pace of mobilisation and brought the end of apartheid within grasp, it also had a militaristic authoritarian culture. In many townships, what the civics said the civics got. If it meant schools were to be closed for an entire year, then the schools would be closed for that period. It was a violent period in our history, with black political parties tearing each other apart in the struggle for ideological hegemony. Many of the people who emerged later as supporters of Zuma came from this period, some of them hardened veterans of the ANC–Inkatha battles in KwaZulu-Natal.

The confluence of the military underground and the militaristic culture of some of the civic organisations became a potent mix that led many people to wonder if we were going the way of many post-colonial societies. Julius Malema's and Zwelinzima Vavi's threats to kill to defend Jacob Zuma sent chills down the spines of many South Africans. Their words seemed to signal the emergence of what Achille Mbembe calls the 'aesthetics of vulgarity' in postcolonial societies. It is a vulgarity that has its roots in the colony. According to Mbembe, the colony exhibits three types of violence. First, there is what he calls the founding violence that establishes the colony. The second is the one through which the state seeks to legitimise itself. However, it is the third type of violence that carries itself through the postcolony. This is the violence that occurs in the most 'banal and ordinary situations', that enables people to laugh at public executions or dance around burning bodies. But the public nature of executions does not serve an idle purpose precisely because 'a public execution not only reveals the total power of the state but becomes a social transaction. The public face of domination can use the execution's threatening implications.' The postcolony becomes an economy of death that 'opens up a space for enjoyment at the very moment it makes room for death'. This is not just violence but violence underwritten by obscenity: 'obscenity, in this context, resides in a mode of expression that might seem macabre were it not an integral part of the stylistics of power'.[13]

Nobel Laureate Wole Soyinka recounts the story of how Nigerian police stopped his friend and fellow playwright Ola Rotimi, his wife and children at a roadblock. The police accused Rotimi of jumping the queue. He was forced to take twelve lashes on his buttocks in front of his family. This form of public punishment often took place at parties if only to send a warning: 'There any act deemed lèse-majesté would result in the open "drilling" of the offender or his kidnapping on orders from the unofficial chairman of the occasion, bloated already by commandeered authority, doubly bloated by ample food, XO Cognac, Veuve Clicquot champagne … and triply bloated by the obsequious attention of his hosts.'[14]

It would be a mistake to limit postcolonial violence to the state. The xenophobic violence in South Africa showed us that the brutality is not the exclusive preserve of the state.

Julius Malema: the underdog must be lumpen to be effective
It would be a stretch of the imagination – and perhaps unfair – to liken Julius Malema to Africa's potentates. As he often says of himself when in a corner, we are youth and we are entitled to be wrong. Many

13 Achille Mbembe, *On the Postcolony* (Berkeley: University of California Press, 2001), 115.
14 Wole Soyinka, *You Must Set Forth at Dawn* (New York: Random House, 2006), 149.

people were of course rightly incensed by Malema's vulgarity. The manner in which he addressed or spoke about people old enough to be his parents or grandparents did not go down well in much of the black community. But the ANC thought differently: it knew that the underdog must present himself as lumpen in order to be effective. While the tendency amongst commentators was to read him the riot act – Meshack Mabogoane called him 'an overgrown child' – Malema became a crowd puller for the ANC, especially among the youth. This was also because there was an element of youth entertainment in Malema's political histrionics. He attracted young people who wanted to come to political meetings to be part of the camaraderie. In the following article I explained Malema as a classic example of the underdog who must, à la Laclau, present himself as lumpenproletariat in order to be effective.[15]

Our criticism of African National Congress (ANC) Youth League leader Julius Malema is misplaced. Societies are by their nature diverse. They throw up all sorts of people – the good, the bad, the nonviolent, the violent, etc.

Much has been made of the fact that Malema did not finish matric. But neither did millions of our young people. The real issue is that we have a political system that makes it possible for such people to assume the leadership of our land.

This is a result of what I once described as a leadership tailspin in the ANC. In 1990 the ANC had its best leadership collective. This consisted of the wisdom of the generation that graduated from places such as Fort Hare in the '30s and '40s (Govan Mbeki, Nelson Mandela, Walter Sisulu, Oliver Tambo); the intellectual brilliance of the exile returnees (Thabo Mbeki, Pallo Jordan, Chris Hani, Zola Skweyiya, etc.); and the political brinkmanship of the mass democratic movement of

15 Xolela Mangcu, 'From Mandela to Malema in three simple steps', *Business Day*, 17 July 2008.

the '80s (Cyril Ramaphosa, Trevor Manuel, Jay Naidoo, etc.).

So formidable was this eclectic leadership collective that it left the National Party negotiators reeling.

However, a tailspin then took place in three stages. First, the wisdom of the older generation was replaced by the showmanship of the exile returnees. The returnees seemed more interested in showing how clever they were than with connecting with the experiences of their people. Thus, under their leadership the life expectancy of the population fell by a whopping 15%.

Second, those who had been in the mass democratic movement were recruited to become part of this charade (Trevor Manuel, Mosiuoa Lekota, etc.), or disappeared from the public stage, Ramaphosa being the most prominent example.

Third, the intellectual pretenders were themselves kicked out in Polokwane by the foot soldiers of the revolution of Jacob Zuma.

Now it would be just a matter of time before the foot soldiers would find common cause with the lumpenproletariat (or what we called 'comrade tsotsis'). There is much that brings the foot soldier and the proletariat together – but mainly it is a strong sense of being underdogs. Lacking in the wisdom of the older generation, the intellectual sophistication of the returnees, and the sense of community of the mass democratic movement, they employ their only comparative advantage – violence.

Nothing gives this group greater satisfaction than seeing members of polite society cringe when it speaks of killing. In *The Wretched of the Earth*, Frantz Fanon describes how the lumpenproletariat enter and occupy the centre of the historical scene: 'So the pimps, the hooligans, the unemployed, and the petty criminals throw themselves into struggle like stout working men. These classless idlers will by militant and decisive action discover the path that leads to nationhood.'

Not only that, they will, in our case, take over the leadership of the nation, wielding the language of violence. From there it is a short jump to either the left-wing populism of the Pol Pot variety or the right-wing populism of the fascist variety. Nowhere in their discourse is there any of the democratic populism we had hoped for in urging them to save us from Mbeki.

So what should be the role of intellectuals at such perilous times? Our experience with Mbeki teaches us that it is precisely when politicians are at their most powerful that we should develop a critical distance from them, for our sake and, more importantly, for theirs.

Vagueness as the new social rationality

One of the most important changes in the political culture of the ANC has been that there became more to politics than what the party calls *umrabulo* (consciousness raising). The new politics seems to be more about aesthetics than substantive arguments. While the educated elite have lamented the lack of content in Zuma's politics, millions have been happy with his symbolic presence on a stage usually reserved for a different set of people. He is the symbol they have been looking for in expressing their disappointment with the establishment. It has not mattered if all he has done is show up to sing and dance for them. It means something to them.

Zuma is a classic populist in the sense of being non-ideological. This is in accordance with Peter Worsley's arguments that populism is not an ideology but 'a dimension of political culture' that cuts across social and ideological differences. This has led to an elite dismissal of populism as simplistic and empty. But Ernesto Laclau argues that the simplicity, emptiness and vagueness are actually the expression of a particular social rationality, which is that people are less ideological than they are often made out to be. It is worth quoting Laclau's view on vagueness as a virtue, partly because Zuma has been criticised precisely for being vague:

Instead of counterposing vagueness to a mature political logic governed by a high degree of precise institutional determination, we should start asking ourselves a different and more basic set of questions: is not the vagueness of popular discourses the consequence of social reality itself being, in some situations, vague and undetermined. And in that case, wouldn't populism be, rather than a clumsy political and ideological operation, a performative act endowed with rationality of its own – that is to say, in some situations, vagueness is a precondition to constructing relevant political meanings? Finally, is populism really a transitional moment derived from the immaturity of social actors and bound to be superseded at a later stage, or is it rather a constant dimension of political action which necessarily arises (in different degrees) in all political discourses, subverting and complicating the operations of the so-called 'more mature' ideologies?[16]

The question this raises of course is, if indeed populism can take on different dimensions – from fascist movements in Europe to popular people's movements in the United States – what direction will Zuma's populist coalition take?

In a recent article for the *Sunday Times*, the director-general in the presidency, Vusi Mavimbela, captures the central contradiction facing the Zuma presidency. The challenge is that of governing with a people whose political culture is steeped in militant and militaristic action: 'the starting point in that evaluation is the recognition of the force of history and culture on the psyche of civil society. The violent practice of defiance and protest that rendered apartheid ungovernable still occupies pride of place in the mind of our civil society.' Mavimbela argues rather perceptively that while the instinct of those in power may be to become defensive and seek to shut down protest action, the real challenge is how to engage such movements: 'the spirit and culture of activism can be redirected by democratizing

16 Ernesto Laclau, *On Populist Reason* (London: Verso, 2005), 17–18.

the very conversation of the struggle of the poor in their quest for access to available and scarce resources. The catchwords here are conversation, inclusivity, engagement and openness.'[17] This is a new and positively encouraging language coming from government. I shall return later to a further exploration of what its elaboration may entail, in both domestic and global politics.

For now I turn to how the elite responded to Zuma's rise. I focus in particular on the triad of law, media and politics, because these institutions themselves must be part of how we re-imagine ourselves. We cannot engage in this collective imagination unless we confront the clash of social rationalities between elite and mass politics in South Africa. The law became the means by which elite rationality would discipline mass irrationality.

17 Vusi Mavimbela, 'New goals, new strategies', *Sunday Times*, 6 September 2009.

3

Politics as law, law as politics: the different cases of Jacob Zuma and John Hlophe

The aim of this chapter is to argue, firstly, that the law has been at the centre of almost all of our major political disputes, with troubling implications for our political culture, and secondly, that political considerations have informed judicial decision-making, with troubling implications for the judiciary. The Jacob Zuma saga over the past decade demonstrates what happens when the law substitutes for politics. The John Hlophe saga demonstrates what happens when politics takes the place of the law. It is not the purpose of this chapter to go into the details of the several legal judgments involving Zuma – or the details of the political arguments in the Hlophe matter – but simply to draw out their implications for our democracy.

I can hardly think of any judicial decisions more consequential for our democracy than those rendered by Advocate Bulelani Ngcuka, Judge Herbert Msimang, Judge Chris Nicholson, Judge Louis Harms and Advocate Mokotedi Mpshe with respect to the corruption charges against Jacob Zuma. Ngcuka's decision not to prosecute Zuma will go down in history as the most controversial legal decision of our young democracy; Msimang's decision to throw the case against Zuma out of court added a spring to Zuma's political step; Nicholson's judgment brought an end to a political era and turned

Zuma's step into a trot for the presidency; Harms's ruling put the brakes on Zuma's campaign and led to the reinstitution of charges against the country's prospective president; while Mpshe's decision led to the revelation of high-level subversion of the rule of law. All of these decisions grappled with the question whether the legal system was being used for ulterior political purposes. More specifically they turned on whether Jacob Zuma was the victim of a political conspiracy led by President Thabo Mbeki or his supporters. The question many asked was whether the successive national directors of public prosecutions – Bulelani Ngcuka, Vusi Pikoli and Mokotedi Mpshe – were pawns in a larger game of political succession. If the national prosecutors could not be trusted to dispense justice without fear or favour, then not only the future of the judiciary but the future of our democracy as a whole was in peril.

The Ngcuka decision (or non-decision)
The history of the corruption charges against Jacob Zuma hardly needs retelling beyond a bare outline. Allegations of corruption in the government's arms deal go back to 2001. The matter shot into the public domain in 2003 when the *Mail & Guardian* published an encrypted fax of a promise to pay R500,000, allegedly to Zuma in return for protection and favours to the French arms company Thales/Thint. At the time Zuma's supporters asked why he had been singled out for investigation when he was not even involved in the arms deal negotiations.[1] They also answered their own question, arguing that Thabo Mbeki was behind efforts to prevent Zuma from succeeding him as president of the ANC and, by extension, from becoming president of the country. These suspicions were further fuelled when in August 2003 the national director of public prosecutions, Bulelani Ngcuka, made a public announcement that

---

1 Andrew Feinstein asked a similar question in *After the Party* (Cape Town: Jonathan Ball, 2007). According to Feinstein the person who presided over the whole thing and therefore had more questions to answer was former president Thabo Mbeki.

although there was prima facie evidence of corruption against Zuma, the state did not have a winnable case and would therefore not proceed against him. Instead the state charged Zuma's 'accomplice' in the act, the Durban businessman Schabir Shaik. It was rather strange that in a bilateral act involving corruption, only one person was charged. After all, corruption involves the person who offers the bribe (the corruptor) as well as the person who accepts it (the corruptee).

After a trial that lasted from October 2004 to June 2005 Shaik was convicted and sentenced to fifteen years' imprisonment. In what turned out to be an embarrassing turn of events, newspapers erroneously attributed to the presiding judge, Hillary Squires, the much-quoted dictum that there was 'a generally corrupt relationship' between Zuma and Shaik. The quote took on a life of its own before the judge emerged from months of silence to deny he had ever said such a thing. Zuma's supporters argued that Squires's clarification showed that in their zeal to find Zuma guilty in the court of public opinion the media had hardly verified their own stories.

On 14 June 2005 President Thabo Mbeki, addressing a joint sitting of the two houses of parliament, fired Zuma from his position as deputy president of the country, in part relying on what the judge had said.

We understand very well that we should at all times act in a manner that seeks to uphold, defend, and respect the Constitution. We have had no precedent to guide us as we consider our response to the judgment by Justice Squires. We have therefore had to make our own original determination on this matter guided by what we believe is in the best interest of the Honourable Deputy President, the government, our young democratic system and our country. I am fully conscious of the fact that the accused in the Schabir Shaik case have given notice of their intention to lodge an appeal. I am equally aware that a superior court may overturn the judgment handed down by Justice Squires. However, as President of the Republic I have come to the conclusion that the circumstances dictate that in the interests of the Honourable Deputy President, the government, our young democratic system, and our country, it would be best to release the Honourable Jacob Zuma from his responsibilities as Deputy President of the Republic and member of the Cabinet.[2]

The Msimang decision

According to the political analyst Richard Calland, 'Mbeki's biggest error was to allow politics and justice to intertwine. Indeed, he started it with his reasoning, back in mid-2005, when he dismissed his then deputy president on the basis of the law – the judgment in the Schabir Shaik case – rather than politics.' Calland argues that by his action Mbeki 'thus linked Zuma's political future to his legal future'.[3] But Mbeki forgot this could play out either way: through the law he could put an end to Zuma's prospects of succession, but if this failed Zuma's political prospects would be immeasurably improved. For all his reputed wisdom, Mbeki never seems to have allowed for the latter outcome.

A week after the president's announcement, the new director of public prosecutions, Vusi Pikoli, instigated corruption charges against Zuma.[4] Once again, Zuma's supporters smelt a rat. Pikoli, who had served as director-general in the Department of Justice, was suspected of being a close Mbeki ally. The case was subsequently transferred from the Durban High Court to the Pietermaritzburg High Court, and the trial date moved to 31 July 2006.

In the meantime there was an ongoing case to decide whether the state had acted legally when it confiscated 93,000 documents from

2 Thabo Mbeki's address to Parliament on 14 June 2005.
3 Richard Calland, 'Where's the "Et tu Brute" moment, *Mail & Guardian*, 10 February 2009.
4 By this time Bulelani Ngcuka had left the public sector for business, although it would emerge years later that he still had a hand in the decision-making processes of the NPA.

Zuma's home and offices. When the Supreme Court of Appeal ruled that the warrants were legal, Zuma appealed to the Constitutional Court. Consequently the state asked for a further postponement of the trial in the Pietermaritzburg High Court pending the outcome of the search and seizure appeal, the outcome of Schabir Shaik's appeal against his sentence, and the outcome of the state's application to the Mauritian authorities to release documents lodged there by the French arms company Thales/Thint.

When the court met on 5 September 2006, the state requested yet another delay but Judge Herbert Msimang would have none of it and ruled that Zuma was being prejudiced by the postponements. Nonetheless, he allowed the National Prosecuting Authority (NPA) to reinstate the charges at a future date. A year later Judge Msimang's decision to dismiss the case against Zuma thus served only to add a spring to Zuma's step as he went into the ANC's leadership conference in Polokwane in December 2007. In fact Zuma used the Msimang judgment as part of his argument that he was being targeted for political reasons. The momentum behind Zuma's campaign has been described by Kgalema Motlanthe:

> Mbeki was lauded for his very high standards. But once you do that, you must live by those standards. You can't lower the bar. You have to be consistent. It simply means that when a whole lot of allegations come up against the national commissioner of police, you could not then respond differently. You could not fail to act in the same way when other members of the Cabinet face other allegations about this and that. If you set the bar, you must live by it. Then there's justice. If it's not that way, then out there the perception takes root that this is an injustice and people rise up against it.[5]

---

5 Kgalema Motlanthe, 'Motlanthe's full-time challenge', *Sunday Independent*, 8 February 2009.

A public debate also ensued about who was responsible for the delays. The insistent question of many journalists and commentators was why Zuma spent so much time and money contesting the state's every move if he had nothing to hide. A similar argument had been raised when President Bill Clinton got the best attorney in Washington, Robert Bennett, to represent him during the Monica Lewinsky affair. The fact is that there is a reason why citizens have a right to legal representation, and that is to protect them from the ever-present danger that the state might take advantage of ordinary citizens. In Zuma's case it would of course turn out that this was exactly what happened.

Zuma's political comeback and the first Mpshe decision

Notwithstanding his legal woes, Jacob Zuma waged one of the most effective political campaigns in modern political history. After his dismissal by Mbeki he issued a statement that he respected the president's prerogative to choose members of his cabinet, although he would later wonder why Mbeki saw it necessary to dismiss him without any charges being laid against him. But this was not such a difficult question to answer. Mbeki most probably fired him in the full knowledge that he would be charged a week later. It is indeed hard to imagine that Vusi Pikoli would have decided to proceed against the deputy president without informing the president.

Zuma then offered to give up all his political responsibilities as deputy president of the ANC. However, leaders of the Communist Party, the trade union federation Cosatu and the ANC Youth League saw in Zuma's case an opportunity to challenge Mbeki openly. Mbeki had hurt too many people and Zuma's cause became the rallying point for the walking wounded in the ANC. Instead of packing his bags and heading for his homestead in Nkandla, Zuma was prevailed upon to fight the good fight. He subsequently crisscrossed the country addressing the party faithful. Matters came to a head at the

ANC national general council (NGC) in June–July 2005. Though the ANC leaders tried to deflect attention from the succession battle by saying this was a policy conference, one of the NGC's most notable decisions was the restoration of Zuma's responsibilities as deputy president of the ANC. The delegates argued that Zuma had been elected to that position by the general membership at an ANC leadership conference, and only that conference could strip him of his powers. This was a reaffirmation of the principle of membership control over the party. It was also the first time that there was a clear public demonstration of anti-Mbeki feeling in the ANC, leading to his ousting at Polokwane.

An important point to bear in mind is that despite his loss of the ANC presidency in December 2007, Mbeki still remained president of the country after Polokwane. He thus attracted the suspicion that he was involved in acting director of public prosecutions Mokotedi Mpshe's decision to reinstitute charges against Zuma barely a week after the Polokwane outcome. Mpshe was acting national director because Mbeki had suspended Pikoli after a warrant of arrest was issued against the national police commissioner and Mbeki ally, Jackie Selebi. Before the Ginwala commission, Pikoli testified that Mbeki had requested him to hold off from executing the warrants for two weeks but Pikoli was not prepared to wait that long. What emerged out of the testimony to the commission confirmed what many had suspected: executive interference in the justice system.

The end of an era: the Nicholson judgment[6]

Zuma approached the Pietermaritzburg High Court in May 2008 to have Mpshe's decision to charge him rescinded. Zuma's legal argument was that in terms of the constitution he should have been invited to make representations when the decision to prosecute him was reinstituted. He said he had a legitimate expectation of being

6 The citations in this section are from the judgment.

invited to make such representations because of what Bulelani
Ngcuka had stated at a press conference in August 2003 in response
to a journalist's question whether the NPA would consider mediation.
'We have never asked for nor sought mediation. We do not need
mediation and we do not mediate in matters of this nature. However,
we have no objection to people making representations to us, be it in
respect of prosecutions or investigations. In terms of section 22(4)(c)
of the Act, we are duty bound to consider representations.'

Zuma argued that the NPA's decision not to invite him to
make such representations before he was recharged was politically
motivated.

On 12 September 2008 Judge Chris Nicholson ruled that Mpshe's
decision constituted a reversal of the earlier decision not to prosecute
and that consequently Zuma was by law entitled to be invited to make
representations. Nicholson also criticised Bulelani Ngcuka's decision
not to prosecute because the concept of prima facie evidence meant
that

> the allegations, as supported by statements and real and documentary
> evidence available to the prosecution, are of such a nature that if
> proved in a court of law by the prosecution on the basis of admissible
> evidence, the court should convict. Sometimes it is asked: Are there
> reasonable prospects of success? The prosecution, it has been held,
> does not have to ascertain whether there is a defence, but whether
> there is a reasonable and probable cause for prosecution.

Nicholson found it odd that after a two-year investigation the state
chose in 2003 not to prosecute under those 'peculiar circumstances'
and instead went to court in 2006 to ask Judge Msimang for a
postponement. This strange behaviour confirmed Zuma's contention
that this was all part of a political stratagem to resurrect the charges
at different moments of the ANC's leadership contest so as to leave

a cloud hanging over his head. Nicholson concluded: 'if one political faction or sectional interest gains a monopoly over its workings, the judiciary will cease to be independent and will become part of a political process of persecution of one particular targeted political enemy.'

Nicholson also lambasted Ngcuka for calling a press conference where he thanked the minister of justice, Penuell Maduna, for his political leadership. The judge argued that the most plausible inference from this was that Ngcuka had sought and received political advice from Maduna. In view of the constitutional independence of the national director of public prosecutions from the executive branch, what did a member of the executive have to do with the prosecution of a person? And why was Maduna at a press conference of the NPA? And why did the decision to prosecute Shaik and not prosecute Zuma require the minister's political leadership? Ngcuka's comments strengthened 'the inference that the decision not to prosecute the applicant was politically driven'.

Although Maduna denied that he had been party to the decision, Nicholson argued that according to the principle of collective responsibility, the cabinet, with Mbeki at its head, was responsible for the actions of both Maduna and his successor as justice minister, Brigitte Mabandla. The judge thus ruled: 'I am therefore not convinced that the applicant was incorrect in averring political meddling in his prosecution.'

Nicholson then laid into Thabo Mbeki for suspending Vusi Pikoli. Mbeki's claim that there had been a breakdown in the relationship between Pikoli and the minister of justice held no water because there should have been no such relationship in the first place, particularly when it came to matters of prosecution. 'The suspension of the National Director was a most ominous move that struck at the core of a crucial State institution.'

Nicholson's judgment was deadly ammunition in the hands of

Zuma's supporters and the 'walking wounded' who were mobilising around him. Daggers were drawn when the ANC's National Executive Committee met on 19 September 2008 in what turned out to be a night-long discussion about whether Thabo Mbeki should be recalled from the presidency of the country. Any such decision would of course have had to go through parliament and there are some who believe that Mbeki might have survived the bruising parliamentary battle. I was one of those outside the ANC who felt that Mbeki posed a continued threat to our democracy. Long before the Nicholson judgment, I made the argument for the president's recall.[7]

There is now near universal consensus that President Thabo Mbeki has been an unmitigated disaster for this country. His erstwhile defenders are nowhere to be seen or heard. There is a part of me that feels vindicated by this sudden realisation, and a part that is angered by it.

Naturally, I support calls for Mbeki to resign or be recalled by the ANC. The man has become an embarrassment and a vexation. But how long should a people take to wake up and speak truth to power? This question will be as relevant under the new group of leaders as it was under Mbeki. For years we watched as the nature of his depredations worsened. There is indeed a qualitative difference between Mbeki's grave policy blunders, and what he is being accused of lately.

In all of my critical writings about his policy faux pas, I never questioned the man's integrity. I just thought he was highly overrated as an intellectual and a political leader. What concerns me about the latest revelations is the possibility that the president may have been deliberately dishonest. It is one thing to be egregiously wrong about public policy but it is simply unforgivable to betray the trust of your people. One reason Richard Nixon will forever stay in ignominy is that he lied to the American people.

Allegations that Mbeki suppressed a critical report about the 2002

7 Xolela Mangcu, 'Finding our voices again after Mbeki', *Business Day*, 15 May 2008.

Zimbabwe elections; ordered a shipment of arms through to Zimbabwe; intervened to protect Jackie Selebi from being prosecuted; claimed that he knew nothing about the allegations against Selebi; or may have improperly benefited from the arms deal, are just of a different order of magnitude from anything I may have written about the man.

A week before Mbeki was recalled, I went to Germany to participate in a colloquium on South Africa at the 2008 Berlin Cultural Festival. On the day of my departure the BBC asked me to respond to a statement by the fiery ANC Youth League leader, Julius Malema, that the National Executive Committee of the ANC was ready to fire Thabo Mbeki at its meeting that forthcoming weekend. Malema had said he even knew how many people would vote for the recall. The BBC interviewer was not giving me any slack. Was Malema's prediction true or false? I put my neck on the line and said it would probably happen. I did not think about the issue for several days while in Germany, until one Sunday morning at breakfast I saw a headline on the internet. My own newspaper, *The Weekender*, had broken the story of Mbeki's dismissal in the small hours of 20 September 2008.

According to those who were at the meeting, the NEC was divided into two. Jacob Zuma was among those who believed that there was no point in forcing out Mbeki only a few months before the next general election. Leading the pack for Mbeki's recall were the respected business leaders Cyril Ramaphosa and Tokyo Sexwale, whom Mbeki had once implicated in a plot to overthrow him. Tokyo Sexwale is reported to have commented that Mbeki did not deserve one more day in office. Just as I had celebrated Mbeki's removal at Polokwane with my friends in Ginsberg, I now celebrated it in the solitude of a hotel room in a foreign country.[8]

8 Xolela Mangcu, 'Bye-bye, Thabo Mbeki, hello democracy', *The Weekender*, 27–28 September 2008.

Good riddance! In any other democratic country, Thabo Mbeki would have been shown the door a long time ago. I personally could not wait to see the back of him. And so when I woke up in a Berlin hotel to learn that we had been 'unharnessed' of the man I screamed at the top of my voice: Yessssss!

My friends sent me messages about how sad Mbeki looked. My response was 'yeah, right, all dictators look sad when they are toppled'. Remember how sad Saddam Hussein and Charles Taylor and Slobodan Milošević were at their trials? Wait until Robert Mugabe gets his comeuppance and you will see how sad he will look.

As for me, I will not shed a tear for Mbeki precisely because he made so many people shed so many tears. I am talking about the preventable deaths from HIV/AIDS while he continued nitpicking as if he could not be bothered by the loss of human life all around him. Zimbabwe became a basket case with his hand-holding of Mugabe. And from across the Atlantic Ocean Mugabe has been shedding tears for his buddy.

The thing is that I believe in root causes. This country is in the muck it is in because of Mbeki's actions – whether we are talking about the persecution of political opponents; meddling in the National Prosecuting Authority's investigations as inferred by Judge Chris Nicholson; the firing and suspension of those who dare to think differently; or that ruinous arms deal.

At the height of his power everyone trembled in the man's presence, and now we are expected to gush in tears at his departure. Not my precious tears. I'll keep them for more deserving candidates – like the friends, relatives and community members I see dying of HIV/AIDS every day because Mbeki would not be bothered.

Why do people overlook Mbeki's gross violations and yet feast on Jacob Zuma's personal failures? A colleague reckons it's elite class prejudice. But it does not make it just or fair. I really shudder to think what would have become of all of us had Mbeki won the third term for presidency of the ruling party.

In the end Mbeki's ousting was good for our country. While other African countries have taken decades to replace one leader, we can boast of having three presidents in 15 years. I don't always agree with Tony Leon but he was spot on when he said that with Mbeki gone 'the ANC cadres and MPs are unlikely to go back to their meek ways. The media and judiciary have also flexed their muscles, after a fairly lengthy slumber during the Mbeki presidency. That is likely to continue and our democracy will be the better for it. The end of Mbeki-ism means politics has changed; the arrogant assumptions of the past have been challenged. South Africa's current uncertainty could, over time, lead to a far less predictable and far more democratic political outcomes.'

Right on, Tony. That is the best thing you ever wrote in all of those years as leader of the official opposition, and it might just prove prophetic. And to my fellow South Africans, think about it this way: would we be in this muck if we had a more democratic, tolerant leader after Nelson Mandela?

The remarkable, and indeed salutary, aspect of Mbeki's ousting was that a president on the African continent was recalled from office without so much as a street protest or a bullet being fired or a movement in the stock markets. People went about their daily routines as if nothing had happened. The spokesperson for the ratings agency Moody's said that they were not interested in individual leaders but in whether there would be policy changes under the new leadership. They also remarked on the fact that this change-over had taken place without any violence. A spokesman for the European Union also commented that they looked forward to working with the next leader. This rather uneventful changing of the guard happened in a continent where it had become the norm for presidents to hang on to power for life. Indeed, South Africa has now had four presidents in fifteen years.

For a few days there was uncertainty about who would lead the country. Would parliament elect Jacob Zuma to take over the presidency immediately and lead the ANC into the elections as president of the country despite the corruption charges against him? Even though the ANC had resolved at its leadership conference in Polokwane that the president of the party should also be the president of the country, the party now made a tactical move. It convened a press conference at which Jacob Zuma announced that deputy president Kgalema Motlanthe would replace Mbeki as president. The official reason was that this was to ensure a smooth transition from Mbeki to Zuma. But the more likely reason is that it would not have been wise for Zuma to take over while the corruption charges were still hanging over him, and also in view of the fact that the NPA had appealed against the Nicholson judgment. In the meantime Mbeki himself was still smarting over Nicholson's decision and decided to join the NPA's appeal.

Zuma in Harms's way[9]

On 12 January 2009 the acting president of the Supreme Court of Appeal (SCA), Judge Louis Harms, gave his ruling on the NPA's appeal to an expectant nation. Harms averred that Nicholson should have stuck to the legal question before him – which was simply whether Zuma was entitled to be invited to make representations before he was charged. He argued that Nicholson had 'overstepped his authority' by introducing political matters that were not before the court. Harms maintained that Nicholson had introduced his personal preferences into the case by calling for a commission of inquiry into the arms deal, by criticising Mbeki's decision to stand for a third term as president of the ANC, and by criticising Mbeki's decision to fire Zuma. By so doing Nicholson 'changed the rules of the game, took his eyes off the ball and red-carded not only players

9 The citations here are from the judgment.

but also spectators'. Harms refuted Nicholson's definition of prima facie evidence by holding that sometimes such evidence may not meet 'the threshold of a reasonable prospect of success'. Contrary to Nicholson's finding, Harms said that Zuma had initially welcomed Ngcuka's decision and did not impute a political motive when the decision was announced.

Harms also differed with Nicholson with regard to the relationship between the minister of justice and the national director of public prosecutions. In his view the minister had to be kept informed of what the prosecuting authority was doing. Even if there were an improper motive, Harms held that 'a prosecution is not wrongful merely because it is brought for an improper purpose. It will only be wrongful if, in addition, reasonable and probable grounds for prosecuting are absent.' Citing the distinguished judge Oliver Schreiner, he said: 'the best motive does not cure an otherwise illegal arrest and the worst motive does not render an otherwise legal arrest illegal. The same applies to prosecutions.'

As to whether Zuma was entitled to be invited to make representations, Harms maintained that Ngcuka had always said that the decision could be revisited if there was additional evidence. The Ngcuka decision was therefore not a decision not to prosecute Zuma 'at any time for whatever crime'. Mpshe's decision to charge Zuma was thus not a review of the Ngcuka decision; it only meant that the Ngcuka decision had been 'overtaken by events'. Moreover, the fact that the case had been struck off the roll by Msimang meant it could not be a review. Technically speaking, there was no case before Mpshe decided to charge Zuma in December 2007.

Harms's ruling was bitter-sweet for Thabo Mbeki. The judge dismissed Mbeki's intervention on the ground that he was not a party to the case. He likened Mbeki to 'a witness whose evidence has been rejected or on whose demeanour an unfavourable finding has been expressed. Such a person has no remedy, especially not by means of intervention.' Unfortunately for Mbeki, the political deed was already done. Harms's ruling would not take him back to the Union Buildings.

The second Mpshe decision and the smoking gun

The Harms ruling meant that Jacob Zuma was now set to lead his party into the elections with charges of corruption still hanging over his head. Zuma announced that he would appeal to the Constitutional Court for a reversal of Harms's ruling. He would argue that his rights had been violated throughout the process, going back to Ngcuka's decision not to prosecute him together with Shaik. With evidence of political interference Zuma would also make representations to the NPA for a permanent stay of prosecution.

But Zuma and his lawyers also had an ace up their sleeve. Zuma's lawyers got access to intercepted conversations between the former director of public prosecutions, Bulelani Ngcuka, and the former director of special operations, Leonard McCarthy. In South African law it is illegal for intelligence authorities to record private conversations without the consent of a judge. The National Intelligence Agency (NIA) had obtained such approval as part of its investigations into whether Leonard McCarthy was involved in illegal activity, in particular his involvement in the so-called Browse Mole Special Report, a document said to implicate Zuma in an attempt to topple Mbeki's government. What remains a mystery is how the intercepted tapes of the conversation between Ngcuka and McCarthy got into the hands of Jacob Zuma's lawyers, which was itself illegal. The only surmise one can make is that someone must have reasoned that it was better to commit a smaller crime to expose a bigger one. Asked about the tapes, the former NIA boss Billy Masetlha said that whoever released them to Zuma's lawyers did not have enough confidence in the NPA or the courts.[10] For years Zuma

10 Billy Masetlha, *Mail & Guardian*, 22 May 2009. Masetlha was suspended and dismissed

had been arguing that the charges against him were part of a political conspiracy, except that he did not have the evidence to prove it. In the *Mail & Guardian* interview Masetlha also made it clear that he had identified the plot against Zuma. He said he asked Mbeki to do something about it but the latter refused:

> I am elated by the fact that it has come to pass that the actual plots [against Zuma] were there ... I went not to the ANC but to the president and said: 'This is happening, you must stop this thing.' If that report to him is ever declassified it will show that I identified the plot, the people behind it, their modus operandi and their plan, which sadly circulated around Zuma. I did that to protect the state, the ruling party and the stability of this country. I have taken an oath of office. I took that information to the president and no one else. I will keep my oath of honour until my grave. We asked the courts to get the president to disclose the report, as part of my defence, but he refused.

Zuma's detractors in the party, particularly Mosiuoa Lekota, had publicly challenged him to provide evidence of a conspiracy or keep quiet. The former justice minister Penuell Maduna had been brutal in his dismissal of Zuma's claim:

> I have noted Accused No 1's claim that the investigation into his alleged involvement in corrupt activities and the subsequent actions by the NPA are part of a political conspiracy to prevent him from becoming President of the country. In particular, I note his accusation that Ngcuka was a participant in such a conspiracy. I reject these allegations in unequivocal terms. I note that Accused No 1 has put up no facts upon which such a serious accusation could reasonably

by Mbeki. He also faced criminal charges with respect to the hoax email saga. The charges were ultimately dismissed by the Pretoria High Court in January 2009.

have been founded, but has chosen instead to rely on rumours, press reports, speculation and innuendo. I am advised that these accusations are scurrilous and unfounded, and that they appear to be part of a concerted publicity campaign.

Maduna argued instead that if anyone was involved in a conspiracy, it was Zuma himself: 'I verily believe that these allegations are part of a cynical ploy by Accused No 1 to evoke uninformed public sympathy and to deflect attention from the serious charges that he faces.'

Judge Harms had overturned Nicholson's judgment mainly because it was based on circumstantial imputations. Now the appearance of the tapes became the proverbial smoking gun in Zuma's legal armoury. They provided irrefutable evidence of what Zuma's supporters had been saying all along about Bulelani Ngcuka. In the tape-recordings, McCarthy referred to a meeting he had with 'the big man' at Luthuli House, otherwise referred to as No 1, and how they were intent on a comeback strategy after the Polokwane loss: 'I am Thabo man. I mean we are still wiping the egg and blood from our faces. We are planning a comeback strategy and once we have achieved that we will clean up all around us.' In another telephone conversation McCarthy also confessed his loyalty to Mbeki: 'you will always be my president.'

For Mpshe the recordings provided proof that the legal process had been manipulated for purposes that were extraneous to the legal issues at hand: 'A fair and just criminal system should not accept the attitude that the end justifies the means ... I have come to the difficult conclusion that it is neither possible nor desirable for the NPA to continue with the prosecution of Mr Zuma.' Judge Chris Nicholson and all those who had suspected a political conspiracy had finally been vindicated.

One of the points Nicholson made in his judgment was the importance of protecting prosecutorial independence. Historically, the role of the attorney-general was seen as part of the political process. The decision to separate prosecutorial decisions was a last-ditch achievement of the white regime in the negotiations of the early 1990s to prevent any new black government from doing what it had done all along. Since then South African jurisprudence has developed with the explicit provision that no person – whether the president or a member of the legislature – can interfere with the decision-making processes of the prosecuting authority. Even though the NPA Act states that the minister has final responsibility, this does not extend to interference with decisions to prosecute or not prosecute. Indeed, the Act provides that 'no organ of state and no member of an organ of state nor any other person shall improperly interfere with, hinder or obstruct the prosecuting authority in the exercise of its duties and functions'.

The question this raises is whether Thabo Mbeki and members of his cabinet were guilty of a crime. But they might also argue that the end of defending Jacob Zuma could not justify the means of releasing tapes illegally to Zuma's lawyers. Whether you are Mbeki's supporter or Zuma's defender there can be no gainsaying that the legal process has been heavily compromised by the political machinations taking place within the ruling party and the state. The tapes revealed what Mpshe described as 'abuse of process'.

Restoring the relationship between law and politics

It would be absurd to argue that there can be no relationship between the law and politics. The law is the expression of a particular set of political values. Speaking at a Nelson Mandela Foundation seminar, Constitutional Court justice Kate O'Regan[11] described the South African constitution as a transformative constitution based on the values contained in the Bill of Rights. Courts and judicial officers are

---

11 Kate O'Regan, 'For life and action: justice, reconciliation and the work of memory', Nelson Mandela Foundation, 2 April 2009.

guardians of that constitution and the values on which it is founded. In her address O'Regan repudiated a legal positivism that would simply lead to judges going along with whatever laws parliament has adopted. The role of judges is to mediate in societal disputes by holding the ground through a reliance on long-established rules of interpretation. Hence Nicholson's argument that judges are not disinterested umpires but administrators of justice. In a *Time* magazine article Edward Lazarus described the role of judges as follows:

> it has become fashionable for nominees to play down their own importance by suggesting that judicial decision making involves nothing more than the simple application of clear, undisputed rules. This is bunk. There is no rule book for constitutional interpretation. In trying to give meaning for such inherently elastic concepts as 'equal protection of the laws' and 'due process', Justices inevitably make subjective judgments that are colored by their individual views about right and wrong, fair and unfair, wise and unwise ... there is a reason Justice Harry Blackmun, a man whose grandfathers idolized Abraham Lincoln, opposed the states-rights movement and was a passionate voice on issues of race. There is a reason Ruth Bader-Ginsburg, a pioneer in the fight for women's legal equality, takes an expansive view of the equal protection clause. And there is a reason Clarence Thomas, who grew up resenting the racial preferences that took him up the educational ladder to Yale Law School, reads the Constitution as imposing absolute colour blindness on government actions. In the hard cases, the political cases, the cases in which constitutional language and history provide no irrefutable answer, judges' formative experiences – family, geography, mentors, and heroes – cleave liberal from conservative and insinuate themselves into the law.[12]

12 Edward Lazarus, *Time*, 8 June 2009.

Constitutional Court judge Albie Sachs has described his latest book, *The Strange Alchemy of Life and Law*, as a reflection of his approach to the law:

So the whole book, if you like, is about subjectivity and objectivity, about how individual personal experiences enter into the objective world of judging, into the public storytelling that judges go in for. It's an argument against the notion that judging is purely rational and purely logical. It's saying that the richness of life experience, the knowledge of what makes people tick, what hurts, heals, unites, divides – these things do come in – although not in an obvious way, and always mediated by legal and collegial culture and always disciplined by legal rigour.[13]

Sachs makes the same argument as Edward Lazarus: 'By definition cases that reach a Constitutional Court tend to be borderline cases, clashing not between right and wrong, but between right and right.'[14]

In his judgment Louis Harms showed hardly any regard for the political and constitutional implications of the state's actions against Zuma. As Justice Leon once noted: 'Experience in many parts of Africa has shown that arbitrary and oppressive use of prosecutorial powers has often been potent weapons of fostering political ends to the detriment and ultimate destruction of democracy. On the other hand, experience, such as that of The Gambia, has also shown that where there is no abuse of prosecutorial powers public confidence in the criminal justice system is maintained.' Clearly, Ngcuka, McCarthy and 'No. 1' acted in a manner that undermined the very values that underpin our constitutional order.

After Mpshe announced his decision not to continue the

13 Interview with Albie Sachs about his book, *The Strange Alchemy of Life and Law* (Oxford: Oxford University Press), *Sunday Independent*, 30–31 May 2009.
14 Ibid.

prosecution of Zuma, he was pilloried in the media. Suffice it to say that in a similar move the attorney-general of the United States, Eric Holder, dismissed a case against the veteran senator Ted Stevenson on the grounds of prosecutorial misconduct. In asking the court to rescind the case and the judgment against Stevenson, Eric Holder said: 'The Department of Justice must always ensure that any case in which it is involved is handled fairly and consistent with its commitment to justice.' This was despite the fact that there was incontrovertible evidence that Stevens had accepted \$250,000 in bribes. In its editorial the influential publication *Slate* lamented the decision thus: 'Holder probably made the right call. But sure it would have been better if he hadn't had to make it. Of course that's the whole point of showing that prosecutorial misconduct won't be tolerated.'[15]

Besides, Advocate Mpshe had done exactly what the constitution enjoins him to do. It requires the national director of public prosecutions to review cases and gives him the authority to decide to terminate them. I made this argument in several columns including the following.[16]

Let's try this one more time: Advocate Mokotedi Mpshe did exactly what the constitution enjoins him to do. In all of the commentary by some of our most esteemed legal scholars and political commentators I still have to come across a rebuttal of this one statement of constitutional fact. You may argue that the decision leaves a cloud hanging over Zuma's head; or that the matter should have been heard by a judge; or that Zuma's possession of the tapes was illegal; or that Mpshe succumbed to undue political pressure with the eye to reappointment by Zuma; or that he acted without regard to the interests of ordinary

15 *Slate Magazine*, 'Eric Holder's bold move in the Ted Stevens case', http://slate.msn.com, 2009/04/01.
16 Xolela Mangcu, 'Ditch the constitution or change your view', *The Weekender*, 11 April 2009.

citizens. You may even hate the colour of his tie or the sound of his voice. Whatever reason you may come up with, there is just no getting around that Mpshe acted within the powers vested in him by the constitution. But just before you despair, you may have one recourse. You can change the constitution – but then again you would have to change the constitution every time you do not like the implications of its provisions. Writing in the *Business Day* the other day, University of Cape Town law professor Hugh Corder argued for 'a judicial crafting of a jurisprudence which gives full effect to constitutional provisions and values'.

Corder was writing in respect of the case of Judge John Hlophe. The interesting thing here is that in acting against Judge Hlophe the Constitutional Court judges have given the exact same reasons as Mpshe. Hlophe, they maintain, interfered with the integrity of the legal process. They do not say he interfered with the evidence in the Zuma matter but that he sought to influence how judges make their decisions.

But is this not exactly what Leonard McCarthy and Bulelani Ngcuka did in influencing the timing of the charges? And this is not a simple matter of timing – as one journo put it. It is 'a simple matter of timing' that is an assault on another person's rights. And if Zuma ever sought to challenge this 'simple matter of timing' he would be accused of acting in bad faith. And so, pardon the pun, a 'simple matter of timing' can take on different meanings depending on which side you are on.

But the person who aptly summed up the whole thing is Lindiwe Sisulu: 'the truth is indivisible ... the head of the NPA said they were misled. You have to wonder where else they were misled.' And that's exactly the point. The NPA could not have prosecuted Zuma, knowing full well that their processes were tampered with. But here I am trying to justify Mpshe's decision when the Constitution does a good job of it. Stop the pretence, folks – we are either constitutional democrats or we are not.

◯

The different matter of Judge Hlophe

If the Jacob Zuma matter was about the use of law to fix a political opponent, the Hlophe matter seemed to be more a matter of using politics to reach particular judicial outcomes. In May 2008 the Constitutional Court issued a media statement to the effect that it had reported Judge John Hlophe to the Judicial Service Commission (JSC) for trying improperly to influence some of its members – Judges Bess Nkabinde and Chris Jafta – to rule in favour of Jacob Zuma in one or more cases that would come before the court. In turn Hlophe laid a complaint with the same body alleging that the Constitutional Court had violated his rights by going to the media with its allegations. He then approached the South Gauteng High Court to ask it to set aside any investigation into his actions on the ground that the JSC, to which the Constitutional Court judges had complained, was not properly constituted and that the members of its complaints committee were biased against him. The court ruled that the Constitutional Court judges had infringed his rights but that the JSC hearing should go ahead as planned.

In the next stage of the drama, the Constitutional Court judges appealed against the High Court decision to the Supreme Court of Appeal (SCA). The SCA in turn upheld the appeal arguing that there was no law that required that the judges should consult him before they laid a complaint against him. Neither had they erred in going public in view of their belief that the independence of the court was being threatened. Having lost the case, Hlophe asked for a postponement of the JSC hearing when he fired his senior counsel, Dumisa Ntsebeza. The postponement was granted but at the next hearing Hlophe did not attend because of a bout of flu, and even after the sick note had expired he asked for yet a further postponement. The JSC decided to proceed without him.

At this point Hlophe brought another suit asking that the whole proceedings against him be set aside. The court ruled that the proceedings should start afresh. This bought Hlophe some time. What is more, four new members were due to be appointed by the president to the JSC and they might prove more sympathetic to his case.

The JSC decided to appoint a three-man subcommittee to hear evidence in the matter and advise its complaints committee whether there was a need for a full inquiry. To the surprise of many and no doubt to Hlophe's relief, the complaints committee announced in August 2009 that it would not be proceeding with a full inquiry into the allegations of misconduct against Hlophe. Even though he had acted inappropriately, his actions did not amount to 'gross misconduct': 'his conduct may have been unwise, ill-considered, imprudent, not thought through, but in and of itself it is not gross misconduct'.

It soon became clear that the JSC's decision was not unanimous and that members were divided on the matter. A minority was of the opinion that the JSC erred in closing the matter without the benefit of cross-examination in a formal hearing. In their view, cross-examination is mandatory when there is a dispute of facts, in this case whether Judges Bess Nkabinde and Chris Jafta were correct in averring that Hlophe had sought to influence them. In other words, it was not up to the accused person but up to the JSC to determine the credibility of the various submissions in a formal hearing. While the majority of JSC members argued that there was no chance that Hlophe would change his position about his intention – 'we would be naïve if we believed that Hlophe will not persist in his denial that he had any such intention, no matter how extensive and intensive the cross-examination' – the minority believed that this was precisely the reason for cross-examination – 'there are disputes of fact which can only be resolved through a formal hearing.'[17]

17 Allister Sparks, 'Zuma must not allow JSC's Hlophe misstep to get uglier', *Business Day*, 2 September 2009.

Is Hlophe a victim of racism?

Like most public controversies in South Africa, the divisions about the JSC ruling took on racial overtones. Allister Sparks argued that 'it has been apparent from the start of this drawn-out saga that there has been a deep reluctance in some legal circles to have a black judge become the first member of the South African bench to be impeached'.[18] The Democratic Alliance also entered the fray by promising to challenge the legality of the JSC meeting at which the ruling was made. It seems that the DA leader, Helen Zille, had received legal opinion that as premier of the Western Cape, the province in which Hlophe is judge president, she should have been part of that meeting. Interestingly, the DA relied on the same technical loopholes it had found unacceptable when others exercised them.

The most vehement critic of the JSC ruling was the former Constitutional Court judge Johann Kriegler. Kriegler announced that he would file a lawsuit in the name of a body called Freedom Under Law, whose members included such prominent black leaders as Archbishop Desmond Tutu, Mamphela Ramphele, Cyril Ramaphosa, Dumisa Ntsebeza and Kgomotso Moroka. While Tutu and Ramphele supported the legal challenge, Ramaphosa, Ntsebeza and Moroka resigned from the body. Ntsebeza accused Kriegler of being patronising to black lawyers and of questioning his abilities. In Ntsebeza's opinion, the way Kriegler talked about transformation was as if there was a necessary trade-off between transformation and excellence in the judiciary. For his part, the political commentator Sipho Seepe argued that Kriegler had used the JSC ruling inappropriately as part of his broader ideological agenda about affirmative action and transformation. Seepe criticised white judges who self-servingly pointed to bad decisions by black judges as 'proof' that excellence had been sacrificed on the altar of affirmative action.

18 Ibid.

In fact, Seepe argued, some of the worst rulings and sentences had been made by white judges.[19]

Among the culprits is the affirmative action beneficiary, now self-styled crusader of excellence, Carole Lewis. She sentenced a man who kidnapped, raped his victim five times and assaulted her, to 16 years because he was employed and 'relatively young'. The rapist was 29 years old. Judge Jeremy Pickering handed down 15 years to a man for raping his six-year-old daughter. The judge said the man acted 'on the spur of the moment' when he brutalised his defenceless daughter. Judge A.J. Visser sentenced Joseph Ntuli to eight years, with four years suspended, for raping a 14-year-old girl twice. Visser put the blame squarely on the shoulders of the victim – he said the victim, 'being the pretty girl she is, might have brought out the animal in the accused'. Judge John Foxcroft sentenced a father to seven years for raping his 14-year-old daughter, arguing that the 'harm of the rape was limited to the victim and not society'. The list goes on. Somehow black judges must assume most of the blame even when the evidence suggests otherwise.

The problem with white-led discussions of the judiciary was brilliantly summed up by Ken Owen in a letter to *Business Day*:

South Africa's judiciary will not be rescued if Judge Johann Kriegler pursues his case, nor will it be doomed if he abandons it. The threat to the rule of law comes from black lawyers who are hustling for jobs, status and power in the name of transformation, and they can be stopped if other black lawyers force them to face up to their responsibility and to the consequences of their rampant ambition. Given our history, whites are wise to avoid preaching to them ... The

19 Sipho Seepe, 'Kriegler's new words crack same old whip', *Business Day*, 9 September 2009.

only useful question to ask is whether black lawyers want the rule of law and are prepared to fight for it; if not there is nothing Kriegler can do about it.[20]

So, yes, to an extent race does matter in the Hlophe matter. But it does not explain everything. We ought to be able to distinguish between Kriegler's patronising attitude towards black people and Hlophe's foolish actions. The existence of racism on the part of whites should never be cause for buffoonery on the part of blacks; otherwise racism would have succeeded beyond Hendrik Verwoerd's wildest dreams.

It would be preposterous to argue that Judge Hlophe's numerous self-inflicted faux pas are a result of white racism. At some point the man must be held accountable for his own actions and utterances, and so must all of us. Although race is a structuring force in our lives, surely there must be room for autonomous decision-making about what is right and wrong in individual conduct. Hlophe has over the years been accused of making derogatory remarks about his colleagues. And then there was the matter of his moonlighting for Oasis Asset Management Company against rules clearly prohibiting judges from earning extra income. Hlophe maintained that the late minister of justice Dullah Omar had given him permission to work for Oasis. Unfortunately Omar is no longer with us to corroborate or deny Hlophe's assertion. Nor has Hlophe covered himself in glory when it comes to his rulings on social issues. In March 2008 he issued a judgment evicting 20,000 shack dwellers from the Joe Slovo settlement in Langa, Cape Town, without any thought as to where these families might be accommodated. In fact he arrogantly refused to give reasons for his judgment. In sum, in the totality of his actions Judge Hlophe has been an embarrassment to the legal fraternity. His pronouncements and actions are hardly the stuff of inspiration for young black kids wanting to become great lawyers.

20 Ken Owen, 'Arrogance isolates', *Business Day*, 15 September 2009.

The JSC is thus to be commended for not rewarding Hlophe's actions by elevating him to the Constitutional Court: he did not make it to the shortlist of candidates for selection. For this reason it would be hard to sustain the argument that the JSC is wholly motivated by racial solidarity in its actions. The best we can say is that race plays itself out in different ways in different situations. When members of the JSC felt they were being treated disrespectfully, some of them may have decided to rally round each other as if to make a collective statement. They were less defensive when they felt at liberty to make their own decisions without 'whites preaching to them'.

The Wits University law professor David Unterhalter responded to the JSC's decision not to proceed with a full inquiry into Hlophe's conduct with a more technical argument. Given its status as the body mandated by the constitution to probe judicial misconduct, it was imperative that the JSC should give 'definitive findings'. 'Anything less casts a long shadow over both the complainant and the judge accused: the complainant because a charge that is made and not sustained on its own terms raises questions about its propriety; and for the accused because charges not properly tested leave doubt, and no judge should be required to stay in office on this basis.'[21]

The problem with Unterhalter's argument is that it places an impossible threshold for unanimity in decision-making. One should expect of this body that members will disagree, just as it is expected of the Constitutional Court. The problem is not one of unanimity but of judgment. Were the majority of members right in deciding that Hlophe's actions did not amount to gross misconduct? Their attitude seems to have been that there was no way of finding this out for sure, not even through cross-examination. But that is where they are likely to have been at fault.

Interestingly, Unterhalter makes a point that differentiates the

---

21 David Unterhalter, ' Divided JSC's ruling leaves damaging legacy for justice', *Business Day*, 3 September 2009.

Hlophe matter from the Zuma matter: 'judging judicial misconduct is altogether unlike judging criminal wrongdoing. We allow, for good reason, a person accused of crime to go free if the state cannot prove its case beyond a reasonable doubt. But a judge accused of misconduct enjoys no such latitude.'[22] Put simply, administrators of justice cannot be allowed to have even the slightest blemish on their integrity. Ironically, the people who make this argument with respect to the Hlophe matter found it hard to accept the very same argument from Advocate Mpshe on the Zuma matter: that administrators of justice must be without reproach.

Conclusion

One lesson to draw from the intersection of law and politics in the Mbeki years is that unless something is done to protect the judiciary from executive interference, the law will be used for political ends. Harms's dictum that 'an improper motive does not otherwise make a legal arrest illegal' has dire implications for our political culture. Suggestions have been made about how to make the prosecutorial function more independent. President Kgalema Motlanthe even proposed that the national director of public prosecutions be appointed by the JSC. While race may have played a part in the decision not to have a hearing, it is hard to sustain the same argument in the light of the JSC's decision against Hlophe's elevation to the highest court in the land. Professional considerations do have a role to play.

The reality, though, is that a ruling party, here and elsewhere, will always seek to influence the operations of the criminal justice system or, as Chartey Quarcoo put it: 'so long as the executive and legislature remain dominated by one party, the NDPP [national director of public prosecutions] may lie at its mercy – in fact, or appearance, both of which impugn the office's reputation for sustained

22 Ibid.

independence.'[23] Things would be different if South Africa were a competitive democracy. Then parliament could fire the president's own appointment or even refuse to confirm his appointments if it felt they were not adequately qualified for the job. Until such time, we are all left to the mercy of the dominant party and the professional conscience of individual members of bodies such as the JSC.

While no ruling party can be expected to appoint judges whose views are likely to undermine what it seeks to achieve, judicial appointments must be informed by the qualifications and experience of the candidates and their standing among their peers. One criterion by which President Zuma will be judged is the extent to which he protects the independence of the judiciary by appointing men and women of integrity to head the courts. The president of the country must therefore set the tone for the judiciary. As citizens we should insist that politicians operate according to the spirit and letter of the constitution.

He must also make sure that, in keeping with the constitution, the judiciary reflects the diversity of the country's demographic profile. His power as president provides him with an instrument to debunk racist assumptions about the relationship between transformation and professional excellence. The constitutional law expert Pierre de Vos has suggested a number of criteria for the appointment of judges to the Constitutional Court.[24] He proposes that the judges must have internalised the values of the constitution, particularly the commitment to social justice and racial transformation. He also argues that 'appointees must demonstrate respect for the separation of powers without kowtowing to any political party. They should be brave and independent without displaying a knee-jerk anti-government attitude.' De Vos further argues that 'appointees must

23 Chartey Quarcoo, 'National Prosecuting Authority: choosing Pikoli's successor a unique chance for reform', *Business Day*, 9 July 2009.
24 Pierre de Vos, 'Appointment to the Constitutional Court', www.constitutionallyspeaking. co.za, 25 May 2009.

have displayed an emotional and academic intelligence, be well versed with constitutional law doctrine, be disciplined and hardworking and, of course, ethically beyond reproach'.

The other lesson to be drawn from this chapter is that while non-racialism is one of the founding tenets of our democracy, we cannot assume that white judges are unaffected by the racism of the society in which they were raised. Nor can we assume that blackness translates into progressive jurisprudence, if Judge Hlophe's career on the bench is anything to go by. It is best to say that at this juncture of our political history our political culture has not reached the level of progress in race matters we could have expected at the founding of our democracy. Fortunately, the legal profession has well-established rules of interpretation to guide them in decision-making. Judges cannot just pass racist rulings and expect to get away with them without the scrutiny of their peers. What distinguishes the legal profession from the media is the manner in which rules of interpretation are entrenched through precedent, appeals and public accountability, at least to the extent that judges must explain their decisions to a broader audience than themselves.

Media entities, on the other hand, operate on the premise that they do not have to account to anyone but themselves, and any attempt to ask them to account for what they publish is regarded as an infringement of press freedom. This lack of public accountability has resulted in unfortunate double standards and a lack of even-handedness. The media were outraged by the abuse of process in the Hlophe matter but were quite happy to ignore it in the Zuma saga. The question is: why?

In the next chapter I argue that the media are just as prejudiced as the society in which they operate. Abuse of process did not matter in the Zuma case because a number of influential journalists and commentators could not be bothered with his rights. It was enough that they wanted him out of the political race. By so doing they conducted themselves in ways not dissimilar to the political hacks who tried to get rid of him by hook and by crook. Those very same journalists are now incensed by the abuse of process in the Hlophe case because they want him out. However, their insensitivity to the abuse of process in the Zuma matter makes it difficult for anyone to take their new-found sensitivity to abuse of process in the Hlophe matter any seriously. Nevertheless, Hlophe may not be the best example of how race and cultural prejudice continue to dog our national institutional life, mainly because his faux pas are of his own making. For a better example we should look at the treatment of Jacob Zuma in the media. As the next chapter reveals, this treatment shows how far in fact we still are from realising our constitutional ideals.

4

The limits of the cultural aesthetic of liberal modernity: how the media were compromised

It is best to say that at this juncture of our evolving nationhood, race and power continue to inform the actions of politicians, judicial officers and the media. The challenge is to develop a critical awareness of these intersections, and how they affect professional practice. Sometimes the interactions are for our collective good – as in building a diverse judiciary – and sometimes they are to our detriment – when they are a cover for prejudice and incompetence.

Over the years I have tended to stay out of discussions of racism in the media. I was not particularly enthusiastic about the South African Human Rights Commission's investigation into the media. This is not to say I was not offended by what I once described as a form of 'media McCarthyism' directed particularly at black intellectuals. One of the most dramatic examples of this was the battle waged by white academics at the University of the Witwatersrand against the distinguished academic Malegapuru William Makgoba. Since then Wits has been unable to retain black academics, many of whom have migrated across the road to the University of Johannesburg. This is rather ironic given Wits's status as a liberal institution and UJ's status as a former Afrikaans university. Although it was always said that racism is a preserve of Afrikaners, many of the institutions that have been dogged by accusations of racism are English-speaking. The post-apartheid experience has demonstrated that universities – particularly the former liberal English universities – have become some of the most conservative institutions in South Africa, as have the English-language newspapers.

Take the *Mail & Guardian*'s treatment of Sam Nolutshungu, an accomplished political scientist at the University of Rochester. In 1996 Nolutshungu was appointed the Vice-Chancellor of Wits. But when he fell ill and declined to take up the position, the *Mail & Guardian* said it was all a lie and accused Nolutshungu of using the Wits appointment to bargain for a promotion at Rochester. A few months later Nolutshungu died of cancer. The same newspaper accused one of the country's leading black intellectuals, Njabulo Ndebele, of embezzling R20 million while head of the University of the North. Similar accusations were levelled at the Vice-Chancellor of the University of South Africa, Barney Pityana. Having falsely presented these individuals as corrupt on billboards across the country, the newspaper would later offer a retraction somewhere in the middle of the paper, leaving unanswered the question how the accused might recover their reputations.

All the same I was still reluctant to see in this a systematic conspiracy by white journalists against the new regime. I was also afraid – yes, afraid – that white journalists would present any official investigation of the media as yet another example of an African government bent on curtailing media freedom. And that is exactly how the Human Rights Commission's inquiry into racism and the media was reported. It did not help matters that the president of the country, Thabo Mbeki, constantly accused the media of racism whenever he was criticised for his absurd policies on HIV/AIDS, Zimbabwe, crime and corruption. It has since emerged that Douw Steyn, a wealthy white South African who was once Mbeki's friend, offered a billion rands to help the government fight crime. Apparently

Mbeki rejected the offer because in his view crime was not the biggest challenge facing the country: it was all a perception mostly shared by whites about an incompetent black government.

It also did not help matters that Mbeki launched a full-scale attack on black commentators, calling them foot-lickers of the white man. His lieutenants were even more extravagant in describing black critics in the media as 'coconuts', 'native assistants' and 'askaris'. I was one of those on the receiving end of the tirades for daring to criticise the president. Perhaps if Mbeki had not conflated his defence of his policy faux pas with charges of racism against his critics, we might have had an opportunity to deal with racism in its own right. And so I believed that patient persuasion and building a moral majority with white colleagues was the way to go. That at least was my argument in the following column.

A couple of years ago a dear friend called me up in Boston, telling me that he was part of a group planning to initiate an investigation into racism in the media. My immediate response was to tell him to 'just forget about it'. I said the media would instead turn their effort into a sensational story about threats to press freedom under a black government. Suffice it to say that my predictions did come to pass. Instead of uncovering stories of racism in the media the Human Rights Commission (HRC) itself became the story. In retrospect I should have suggested a two-pronged approach to my friend – one that differentiated between overt racism and involuntary stereotyping. For even if both manifestations of racism are equally demeaning to their victims, they nonetheless require different policy responses. On the one hand, the law should take its course in prosecuting overt racist actions that violate our anti-discrimination laws. On the other hand, public morality can be brought to weigh on those who refuse to abandon their involuntary stereotypes. If we don't make the distinction between overt racism and involuntary stereotyping, then decent journalists who make involuntary mistakes could find themselves tarred with the career-ending label of racist.

But this differentiated approach has its own problems as well. Real racists could always ascribe their actions to involuntary mistakes. And just as they can hide behind 'involuntary' mistakes, they can always invoke arguments about freedom of expression as a subterfuge to avoid scrutiny. Indeed, arguments made in the name of freedom of expression increasingly resemble a moral relativism that makes no moral distinction between racist and nonracist reporting – we should leave everything to individual journalistic taste.

Given these problems of potential evasion, why should the HRC even consider such a differentiated strategy? From a strategic viewpoint this approach could build a critical mass of support and allies for the HRC's work within the domain of public opinion. Where the necessary legal means have not been successful – as with the subpoenas to editors to appear before the HRC – the human rights body can always appeal to public morality to achieve its ends in cajoling the media to free itself of racism. Even though they have won the battle over the subpoenas the editors still have to win the war of public opinion and media credibility. It is in their interests to protect their individual and collective self-image. Nothing induces change in corporate behaviour like bad publicity and a diminishing bottom line. Ask the chain restaurant Denny's what happened when it was found to discriminate against black people in the United States.

But above and beyond these strategic calculations, both the HRC and the editors should strive towards a common understanding of the role of the press in our society. Contrary to the moral relativism that dominates discussion of press freedom, we need to understand that freedom of expression was never a value-free concept. It came out of eighteenth-century normative struggles for civil rights in Europe. In South Africa, too, freedom of speech must be located within broader normative struggles for the equal treatment of all individuals and communities with dignity and respect. What we should be striving for is a moral pluralism that upholds certain non-negotiable moral values such as antiracism – even if we accept that not every journalist will be converted into a nonracist. The noted democratic theorist Michael Walzer once wrote that a democracy requires a people with thick skins – people who can defend the rights of others to be as despicable as they wish as long as they do not break the laws or harass others to be like them or expect the society to fund their projects: 'they can be permitted only a sectarian existence.' If the HRC is to adopt a more expansive and differentiated approach to media racism, it will need the cooperation of the editors in permitting the racists in their midst only a sectarian existence.[1]

Ten years later I wonder if my cautiousness was not a form of denial in its own right. My eyes were opened when I started writing in defence of Jacob Zuma against some of the most prejudiced and bigoted attacks in the media. Now it was not black radicals who were calling me names. It was my fellow journalists and commentators. I was even lambasted for criticising the hand that fed me – in other words, for being ungrateful for the space I had enjoyed for a full ten years. The cartoonist Jonathan Shapiro published a cartoon labelling me and other journalists and commentators 'previously sensible individuals'. What struck me about this was the sense of entitlement and authority with which such labels were dispensed: sensible by whose standards?

This question about standards got me thinking that perhaps this was what was happening to Zuma – that an elite segment of society has taken upon itself the role of arbiter of social, political and intellectual behaviour. There was no sense that within our democratic space there was room for disagreement about political issues. The logic in

1 Xolela Mangcu, 'Racists in the media must be restricted to a sectarian existence', *Sunday Independent*, 3 May 2000.

the media, particularly the newspapers, seemed to be that you were sensible for as long as you were on 'our' side and unreasonable the moment you were on 'theirs'.

In his classic work, *Public Opinion*, Walter Lippmann captured the role of prejudice in the media as follows:

> In the great booming, buzzing confusion of the outer world we pick out what our culture has already defined for us, and we tend to perceive that which we have picked out in the form stereotyped for us by our culture ... no wonder then that any disturbance of the stereotypes seems like an attack upon the foundations of the universe. And where big things are at stake we do not readily admit that there is a distinction between our universe and the universe. A world which turns out to be one in which those we honor are unworthy, and those we despise are noble, is nerve-racking. There is anarchy if our order of precedence is not the only possible one.[2]

Newspaper reportage of Zuma's legal and political tribulations became a classic illustration of the maxim that 'a world which turns out to be one in which those we honor are unworthy, and those we despise are noble, is nerve-racking'. It was precisely because any conception of Zuma as having any virtues was 'nerve-racking' that critics used the fullest might of their pens to denigrate him. This was essential if we were to preserve 'the order of precedence' bequeathed us by history with all its stereotypes. The stereotypes played an essential role in a country where individual self-esteem has come to depend on putting others down, on account of their race, class, gender, ethnicity, religion or country of origin.

While I still cringe at the race prejudice that informs much of the writing on Zuma, I still believe that racism is just but one part, even if a major part, of the story. This is not to deny the existence of

2 Walter Lippmann, *Public Opinion* (New York: Free Press, 1922), 55.

racism but simply to problematise its discussion. This means that as blacks we cannot explain all of our individual actions in terms of racism. In the white world it means we cannot deny the persistence of racism even among so-called progressives. There is indeed one major difference between my position on race ten years ago and now. I am now no longer willing to assume that the majority of my white colleagues in the media are part of the progressive moral majority I wrote about back then. The racist writings on Zuma, and the silence from white colleagues, have shattered my assumptions about the non-racial consensus that I believed existed.

But why is race not the entirety of the story then? In the hands of black journalists the lenses of class, culture and education played an equally bigoted role in our treatment of Zuma. And so I have chosen to describe the prejudice against Zuma in terms of a 'cultural aesthetic of a non-racial liberal modernity'. We could not bear the idea of Zuma as president because he was not like us – and by 'us' I mean the black and white educated elite who wrote editorials and newspaper columns on a daily basis. Zuma became an affront to the decorum of our world. Instead of speaking in polished tones or citing great philosophers, his speech was most ordinary. And to our eternal embarrassment the man dances in public to throngs of people. 'How uncivilised!' we murmured to ourselves in self-congratulatory indignation.

But it is precisely because we saw him as existing outside our world that we would not accord him the respect we gave Mbeki. Even if we hated Mbeki's politics and his policies he was still one of us, a consumer of fine tobacco, fine Scotch and good old English sartorial elegance. I was also taken aback by the prospect of an uneducated traditionalist assuming the leadership of our nation. 'It had never happened before, why now?' I demanded of the nation in a *Sunday Times* article.[3]

3 Xolela Mangcu, 'If dignity prevails, so will Tokyo', *Sunday Times*, 27 May 2007.

In the 1980s the international community looked with anxious anticipation at whether P.W. Botha would cross the political Rubicon and bring about fundamental political changes. Botha missed the historical moment and the task fell to his successor, F.W. de Klerk. A quarter of a century later, the black community is faced with its own Rubicon. We are faced with a stark choice between the low road and the high road. The low road is represented by those who, in the name of Jacob Zuma, claim to be the natural guardians of this society. They bully everyone into submission with militaristic politics reminiscent of the worst periods of the 1980s. I hear their shrill voices and say to myself: 'We have been here before.'

I do not think there is any commentator who has been fairer to Zuma than I have. I have refrained from commenting on his guilt or innocence, arguing insistently that that should be the province of the courts. In article after article, I counselled the ANC to find a political solution to the matter. However, Zuma has brought a political solution without much help from the ANC or anyone else. By his own actions he has turned his campaign into a 'theatre of the absurd'. It is one thing to make a mistake, but quite another to display a congenital proclivity to self-destruction. One moment he is talking about taking a shower after sex to prevent contracting HIV, the next moment he is an honorary priest, then it turns out his advisers cooked up a hoax assassination attempt. Whether he was complicit in that story has yet to emerge. But one does not have to believe in Zuma's guilt or innocence to reach the conclusion that the man is out of his depth in the high-stakes game of representational politics. After all, leaders are the embodiment of our aspirations. We expect that they should carry themselves with grace and dignity. They should be carriers of the finest ethical traditions of their political movements and societies.

Part of the attraction of ANC leaders such as A.B. Xuma, James Moroka, Albert Luthuli, Oliver Tambo, Nelson Mandela and Thabo Mbeki is that they were or are gentlemen in the finest sense of that term, carrying themselves with grace and dignity. The same holds for those other eminent gentlemen of the revolution, Robert Mangaliso Sobukwe and Steve Biko.

I respectfully submit that Zuma's public actions are an assault on that sensitivity. I become embarrassed for black people whenever Zuma gets on with his song and dance. The song and dance is a form of narcissistic self-validation for the actors behind his campaign. Their vim and vigour are matched only by an unremitting rage against those who regard themselves as the black mainstream. The air is always heavy with violent militarism whenever these folks get into their trance. Achille Mbembe writes menacingly about this production of 'burlesque'. The burlesque shows itself when 'in their desire for a certain majesty, the masses join the madness, and clothe themselves in cheap imitations of power to reproduce its epistemology, and when power, in its violent quest for grandeur, makes vulgarity and wrongdoing its main mode of existence'.

Zuma is a powerful man who, through word and deed, seems bent on making wrongdoing the main mode of his political existence. Excess, spectacle, and militarism have become his only mode of political articulation. And the black mainstream cowers and runs for cover. But there is also something at play in this mainstream collusion with Zuma's antics. Mbembe calls it conviviality. Conviviality is neither acceptance nor rejection but simply playing along. Those who laugh and play along are neither accepting nor rejecting of JZ. They are simply bearing witness.

I have been in meetings where JZ sings 'Umshini wam'. The power of the song is irresistible, and so you lose yourself in the hilarity of the moment. But the hilarity can never be a substitute for political deliberation about the kind of leadership this society needs.

This brings me to the high road of the black mainstream. This high road is not a matter of class or education or anything of the sort. It is a quality that I used to see in my mother (who was well educated) and Steve Biko's mother (who was hardly educated). They were indistinguishable in their grace, dignity and sense of self-worth. Those are the qualities I want to see in my leader. As Cornel West puts it, 'people, especially poor and degraded people, are also hungry for meaning, identity, and self-worth.' For all his faults – and there have been many – Mbeki has always carried himself with grace and dignity and self-worth. With Mbeki you never get a sense that the crown fits uneasily. On the contrary, the crown fits so snugly that the man seems reluctant to take it off and pass it on.

Over the past three years I have suggested that people like Mosiuoa Lekota, Pallo Jordan, Kgalema Motlanthe and Tokyo Sexwale could fill Mbeki's shoes. I would choose any of these individuals over the spectacle of a Zuma presidency. But in a democracy we go with the leaders we have. As it happens, Sexwale is the only man standing as a representational embodiment of the sense of grace, dignity and self-worth that has always been the defining characteristic of the black world. The question is whether that ethic of respectability has any place in the ANC of today. If it still exists, then those who represent it are spectacularly silent in the midst of militarism and the bellicosity of the Zuma campaign.

In my thinking at the time I had substituted my own cultural aesthetic values and ethic of respectability for that of the people of this country, to whom Zuma remained a representational hero. Many of those people saw in him someone who looked, talked, acted like them and empathised with them. What I forgot was that black people were not as judgmental and unforgiving as many of us in the media. If that were not the case, we would not have had a peaceful transition from apartheid to democracy. But people in general are willing to look beyond the flaws of an individual in ways that are not obvious to the unforgiving culture of the chattering classes. They see values such as modesty and accessibility and contrition as much more important than the grace, sophistication and dignity that I was hankering for in my article. Or, put differently, their sense of dignity is not dependent on the artifices of modernity or what Cornel West called 'the felicities of bourgeois existence'.[4]

But my response was mild compared with what other writers had to say about Zuma. The editors of the *Sunday Times* (Mondli Makhanya), the *Financial Mail* (Barney Mthombothi) and *City Press* (Mathatha Tsedu) were scathingly critical of Zuma. To them he was an unmitigated disaster and a crook to boot. In that respect they also shared in the aesthetic of liberal modernity that saw Zuma as an affront – as a corrupt, uneducated polygamist with no place in the modern world. Zuma represented the end of civilisation as we had come to know it. One writer, Prince Mashele, even went so far as to assure everyone that doomsday was upon us and white people were about to be attacked in Cape Town by Jacob Zuma's supporters in MK's Veterans Association.[5] Mashele's article was published in the *Sunday Times* just before the Association planned a march in protest against Western Cape premier Helen Zille's remarks that Zuma threatened to spread HIV among his wives. What convinced Mashele that blood was about to flow in the streets of Cape Town was the use of the word 'ungovernable'. That word had led to a loss of life in the 1980s, and this is exactly what was to be unleashed on white folks this time round. So bent was Mashele on working up racial emotions that it did not cross his mind that disgruntled soldiers might one day march on Jacob Zuma himself, demanding wage increases.

What was interesting about white journalists and commentators was that they prefaced their remarks or defended their prejudiced writing by pointing to their struggle credentials. This touches on my earlier point that we often assume that the English-speaking section

4 Cornel West, 'Nelson Mandela: great exemplar of the grand democratic tradition' in Xolela Mangcu (ed.), *The Meaning of Mandela: A Literary and Intellectual Celebration* (Cape Town: HSRC Press, 2006), 18.
5 Prince Mashele, *Sunday Times*, May 2009.

of the white community was innocent of racism. Now, there is an unspoken rule in journalism that we are not supposed to criticise each other, for reasons that still escape me. It's alright for us to lampoon politicians and members of the public but we are not supposed to take each other on. It's one of those corporate things I can never understand. But in many instances I felt compelled to respond to some of the bigoted writings of my fellow columnists. And when the offensiveness of their language is pointed out, they complain that they are being 'attacked'; and it is at this point that their struggle credentials are brought out. The assumption is that black readers keep a checklist of which journalists were in the struggle.

I am not calling for self-censorship in writing about black politicians. But I believe that a greater sense of self-awareness about language and the context in which it is interpreted could improve journalistic practice. Here are some of the most offensive examples to appear during the Zuma saga.

In September 2008 Jonathan Shapiro (aka Zapiro) published a cartoon in the *Sunday Times*[6] in which he portrayed Zuma as well as Zwelinzima Vavi and Gwede Mantashe about to gang rape a woman whom he depicted as 'Lady Justice'. This cartoon caused such revulsion in the country that Zuma filed a lawsuit against Zapiro. In response, the cartoonist hid behind the well-worn defence of freedom of expression. But surely freedom of expression does not exist in abstraction and outside any consideration for other people's rights? But Zapiro could not be bothered, for his right to freedom of expression trumped Zuma's right to dignity. And it did not matter to him that Zuma had been acquitted by a court of law of rape. This was the irony of it all. As I argued in the column below, the very same people who argued for the rule of law would not accept the decisions of the courts. I also asked what made Zapiro's vulgarity any more acceptable than Julius Malema's.

6 *Sunday Times* cartoon appeared on 7 September 2008.

I have been racking my brain trying to figure out why Shapiro's vulgarity is deemed more acceptable than Julius Malema's 'kill for Zuma' call. Could it be that Shapiro is a cartoonist who uses metaphors to get his points across? Could it be that as a journalist he enjoys freedoms and immunities that Malema does not? Or could it simply be that Shapiro is white and Malema is black?

Let us explore each of these hypotheses in turn. The argument that Shapiro's cartoon is a metaphor for what is happening to the justice system is the weakest. If Shapiro is entitled to metaphors, then so is Malema. Shapiro tried arguing that the cartoon had nothing to do with Jacob Zuma's rape trial. If anything, that response showed his contempt for the thinking public: the cartoon itself is the ultimate artistic expression of contempt for this society, its institutions and its values.

The cartoon is defended in the name of a warped notion of freedom of expression that arrogates to journalists the right to insult and demean others, while at the same time using that same notion as a defence against being demeaned and threatened by the likes of Malema. In that sense journalists want to have their cake and eat it.

But is it not ironic that the same Shapiro, who pretends to defend the justice system, actually mocks that system's acquittal of Zuma on rape charges in this cartoon? The hypocrisy lies in the fact that not once did Zuma ever defy our courts or mock their decisions the way Shapiro has done in this cartoon. It is Shapiro who is resorting to extra-judicial tactics, not Zuma.

And what should we make of the argument that this is critical art at its best? I was never trained as an artist or a journalist. But is there anything in art or journalism school that demands that criticism should amount to the debasement of other people? Has Shapiro stopped to think that on the other side of his drawings is a human being, with children and grandchildren? Has he stopped to think that it is when people are stripped of their dignity they resort to dangerous reprisals?

This brings me to the matter of race. The cartoon appears within the context of a series of articles that are simply contemptuous of black people. The cartoon is a recycling of the age-old racist stereotype about the uncontrollable, sex-crazed black male. What business does a family newspaper have carrying this stuff? And what are our children supposed to make of it – that their leaders are a bunch of gang rapists? And even if you do not want to accept the Zuma acquittal, on what basis can you infer that Gwede Mantashe and Zwelinzima Vavi and others in the cartoon are gang rapists?

I saw that cartoon and felt ashamed of being associated with an industry that debases people in this manner. What happened to empathy for other people, however disagreeable we may find them? Isn't that, after all, the gift of Nelson Mandela – who found some good even in the most racist criminals? Or is that a gift that only white people deserve, while people such as Zuma are undeserving of any modicum of respect as human beings?

Shapiro may disagree with Zuma but he is not entitled to demean his humanity. The cartoon reminded me of what Njabulo Ndebele once described as 'the desecration of black bodies in present-day South Africa'. He called for a 'shift in white identity in which whiteness can undergo an experiential transformation by absorbing new cultural experiences ... An historic opportunity has arisen for white South Africans to participate in a humanistic revival of our country.'

There is a certain mob psychology about Zuma in the media and among the so-called elites that I find frightening. The only problem is that mob psychology only begets mob psychology. This is a long way of saying there is a race war waiting to happen in this country, and people such as Shapiro will have played no small part in fanning the flames.[7]

7 Xolela Mangcu, 'Zapiro cartoon mocks what it pretends to defend', *Business Day*, 11 September 2008.

Rhoda Kadalie echoed my concerns in a letter she published in the press.

Xolela Mangcu stylishly demolishes Zapiro's vulgar cartoon and exposes it for all the diabolical prejudices embedded in it ('Zapiro cartoon mocks what it pretends to defend', September 11). So many people wanted Jacob Zuma to be found guilty of rape, just to complete their racist picture of someone who is a traditionalist and polygamist.

When he was acquitted, they continued with the accusation because they could not afford to have their prejudices destabilised by even a legal judgment. In this, many feminist and racist prejudices concur. Zapiro's cartoon is gratuitous, and to justify it on the basis of freedom of expression is to give respectability to his own base motives. I often wonder why he wins awards because he is actually a cowardly cartoonist, selective in his choices as to whom to ridicule.

I once challenged him to bludgeon the Palestinians as much as he does the Jews, and he simply kept schtum![8]

At the same time Sipho Seepe saw in Zapiro's cartoon a reflection of the herd mentality in the white journalistic fraternity when it came to Jacob Zuma. 'Zapiro may wish to heed Kofi Annan's advice that cartoonists should consider how their work is seen and felt by different groups of people. He noted that cartoonists "can encourage us to look critically at ourselves, and increase our empathy for the sufferings and frustrations of others ... they can use their influence, not to reinforce stereotypes or inflame passions, but to promote peace and understanding."'[9]

In his column in the *Sunday Times*, Mac Maharaj had this to say about Zapiro's condescension:

8 Rhoda Kadalie, 'A coward, I say', Letter to *Business Day*, 15 September 2008.
9 Sipho Seepe, 'The encroachment of white supremacist thinking', *Business Day*, 5 May 2009.

When Zuma was inaugurated, Zapiro was candid. He would keep the shower head in his cartoons. Adverse reaction forced him to retreat. In the tradition of the fearsome schoolmaster of yesterday, he condescended to remove it on pain of good behaviour by Zuma. Without a blush on his cheeks he set himself up as judge and executioner with the threat of the shower head as a symbol of his power.[10]

The reaction to Zapiro among black people became explicitly racial. This was the case after the *Sunday Times* published another one of Zapiro's cartoon in which he depicted me, Sipho Seepe, Pallo Jordan, Karima Brown and others receiving his shower. The cartoon had the caption 'previously sensible individuals'.

In yet another example of stereotyping Jonny Steinberg used a sexual metaphor to describe why young black males were voting for Zuma.[11] According to Steinberg, the reason Zuma was so popular among young black males was that many of them were sexually dysfunctional, and they saw in Zuma a symbol of male sexual virility. Steinberg's article starts with a description of a visit to the Transkei where he had been shadowing some doctors:

> During the early stages of Mbeki's decline and Zuma's rise, I spent a great deal of time in the old Transkei... I shadowed several doctors as they went about their work: in the end, about 12 of them. Without exception, each had young men come to them with a sexual complaint. 'Doctor, there is something wrong with my penis,' these young men would typically say. 'It isn't working properly.'

Steinberg then says the story has 'political ramifications that are

---

10 Mac Maharaj, 'Could it be that many in the media got it wrong', *Sunday Times*, 22 August 2009.
11 Jonny Steinberg, 'Of blocked paths, borrowed dreams and Zuma's appeal', *Business Day*, 18 May 2009.

deeper than may appear at first blush'. The deeper meaning is that Zuma could be a sexual opiate for many of these young people. And then he denies what he affirms: 'I am not saying that poor young men voted for Zuma in droves simply because he sleeps with, and, if he is to be believed, pleasures, many women. It's far more complex than that.' And the affirmation:

> voting for Zuma becomes a little like the trip to the doctor. The young man in the voting booth is taking a pill, an opiate, to be precise. He has forgotten, for a moment, that he does not have work meaningful enough to give him pride, and that he will not have children who bear his name. One can only hope and pray that this is not what voting for Zuma comes to mean. Young men do not thrive on opiates for long. They will soon want much more from Zuma than a borrowed dream of sexual prowess.

Once again, can anyone imagine a black columnist writing something like this about a white politician as a symbol of white pathology? And on what evidence does Steinberg reach his conclusion? Did he perhaps conduct an exit poll that might lead him to think Zuma's sexual virility was a factor in the voting booth for all the young black men who voted for him? But then again he can say all these things in the name of freedom of expression. And I am sure he could produce his struggle credentials as his defence armour. But as Steve Biko once put it, 'the biggest mistake the black world ever made was to assume that whoever opposed apartheid was an ally.'[12] Interestingly, none other than the great liberal Ken Owen invoked Biko in his description of Jonny Steinberg. According to Owen, Steinberg displays 'the kind of unconscious racial arrogance that in my experience drives people to fury'. Owen was reacting to Steinberg's argument that had white people been more involved in

12 Steve Biko, *I Write What I Like* (Johannesburg: Picador, 2004), 68.

Zimbabwean politics, the collapse of that country might have been averted. Invoking Steve Biko and Malcolm X, Owen concluded: 'Certainly it is time to shed the idea that black people can only be successful (or prosperous, or happy, or free, or brave) if whites do something, or refrain from doing something.'[13]

Turning jurisprudence on its head: guilty until proven innocent

The passionate responses that Zuma evoked led members of the media to violate some of Western society's most cherished values and some of our own constitution's prescriptions. Anton Harber opened the debate by questioning whether Zuma was entitled to the protection of the well-established jurisprudential principle of innocent until proven guilty.[14]

> Every now and then, there is a need to challenge a notion that has become so commonplace that it is repeated again and again, even though it is patent nonsense. One of these is the idea that we are obligated to presume a person innocent until proven guilty. Presidential nominee Jacob Zuma wants to be presumed innocent, even though there is evidence pointing to his guilt. But outside of the courts we don't, can't and shouldn't presume someone is innocent when the evidence is otherwise, particularly if we are trusting them with authority, power and public resources.

Harber then disparaged the presumption of innocence principle as a legal fiction that did not necessarily coincide with the facts. Ordinary citizens, he contended, were not duty-bound to follow such a fiction. After offering a number of examples in which we treat strangers, such as the technician who comes to fix the phone in our

---

13 Ken Owen, 'Arrogance isolates', *Business Day*, 15 September 2009.
14 Anton Harber, *Business Day*, 4 March 2009.

house, as guilty until they prove their innocence, Harber argued that we should extend this distrust to politicians:

So why do politicians think that we should act differently when it comes to them? Why do they expect us to place or retain them in high office on the legal fiction that they are honest instead of satisfying us as a fact that they are? Why do they insist that we rely upon legal fiction rather than telling us the facts?

Harber then reveals his journalistic philosophy:

the journalistic fiction is a presumption of guilt. I tell aspirant young journalists to assume anyone with power is lying and guilty. The last thing you want a young reporter to do is accept the word of authority at face value. Their job is to disbelieve and question. They know it is a fiction. They know that some politicians are honest sometimes. But if you assume they are not, you start asking useful questions.

The same argument was repeated by David Beresford in an article also published in *Business Day*.[15] According to Beresford, the presumption of innocence should not be taken as meaning that the defendant is innocent. While affirming the principle as 'one of the fundamental tenets of the legal system', Beresford turned round to argue that it is 'merely an assumption' made for the convenience of the courts: 'as an extreme example, if Adolf Hitler were to be found alive tomorrow, cowering in some jungle hideout, he would enjoy – so far as the courts are concerned – an assumption of innocence until brought to trial. But there would be no need to restore him to the Chancellery pending his trial.'

An extreme example indeed, but does anyone really think the two

---

15   David Beresford, 'Reasonable doubts about the man who would lead SA', *Business Day*, 30 March 2009.

are comparable? But Beresford proceeds undeterred, arguing that while the presumption of innocence may be relevant in the courts, 'it can co-exist with a presumption of guilt on the part of the rest of society. For the sake of the law, we will assume Zuma's innocence. But outside the courts the citizenry may well conclude that the anticipation of a "guilty" finding is what accounts for his reluctance to be brought to trial.'

Yet another distinguished journalist, Allister Sparks, also found the principle of innocent until proven guilty rather inconvenient.[16]

> So, eight years after this legal saga began, and after countless court actions in what became known as Zuma's 'Stalingrad strategy' of delay, he will be freed without a public trial. He will remain forever 'innocent until proved guilty' in circumstances where there was no trial in which that could be tested. But he will not have the opportunity to clear his name either. In legal terms this doesn't count, for the presumption of innocence must stand. But in politics, perceptions are everything and, as a recent opinion poll indicated, the majority of ANC members themselves don't believe Zuma is innocent. Nor do nine out of 10 whites, coloureds and Indians.

It's not clear to me where Sparks got his numbers, but somehow what African people, not just ANC members, think is somehow conspicuously missing from his statistics. This proves yet again that statistics can be manipulated to say whatever you want them to say. As the saying goes, 'there are lies, damn lies and statistics.' And yet for many Africans Jacob Zuma was a victim of the machinations of power and prejudice. But if it were up to Harber, Beresford and Sparks, Jacob Zuma would have been hanged in public a long time ago because only their opinions matter: Zuma was the equivalent

16 Allister Sparks, 'Lost, arrogant ANC needs swift kick from electorate', *Business Day*, 1 April 2009.

of Adolf Hitler, finish and *klaar*. The very same people who called for Zuma to go on trial because everyone should be treated as equal under the law argued that he should be treated differently because he is a politician. In their view the standard by which he ought to be judged was public opinion. A prejudice against politicians was being expressed as a statement of fact and given a veneer of respectability under the guise of freedom of expression. I responded to the dangers to the rule of law posed by this kind of journalism.[17]

During one of our weekend fireside chats a friend said something I hope starkly illustrates the peril that our media pose to our democracy. The subject was what to make of the growing cynicism amongst some of our journalists about the common law principle of 'innocent until proven guilty'. My friend asked: 'Would your journalist colleagues accept it if we presume them guilty of racism with respect to Jacob Zuma? Would they accept that it is now up to them to prove their innocence?' Now, I am one of those who argued that subliminal racism against my white colleagues would be almost impossible to prove. But now thanks to those same white colleagues there would be no need to prove anything. This is the problem when you twist and turn venerated principles for your convenience. Today it may be Zuma, and tomorrow it could be you and me.

And why do I think that the same journalists who demand Zuma should go to court would not accept the court's decision if he were to be acquitted? I bet you they would insist he was acquitted on account of his powerful position. Nothing short of a conviction would satisfy them. Besides, why would journalists who have refused to accept Zuma's acquittal in the rape case accept his acquittal in the corruption trial? The prejudices are just too deep-seated for such an about-turn ever to take place.

17 Xolela Mangcu, ' What it is about Zuma that is driving this fraternity nuts', *Business Day*,
     2 April 2009.

However, I still do not think the prejudices are just racial. Some black writers have produced equally scathing articles against Zuma. That is par for the course in a democracy. What I have objected to is the foulness of their language. Surely we can disagree without swearing at each other?

One of the more interesting developments is the attempt to retrieve and rehabilitate the discredited 'fitness to govern' argument. So promiscuous is this concept that people with as varied political outlooks as Anton Harber, Thabo Mbeki, Frene Ginwala, Kgalema Motlanthe and Ronald Suresh Roberts have used it to defend their political positions. There is indeed nothing as unilluminating as saying that someone you don't like is not fit for office. Duh! The reason we vote against our opponents is precisely because we think they are not fit for office. So why not let the voters decide on Zuma's fitness or lack thereof? Oh, I can hear the argument coming. If we had a system of directly electing our leaders, then we would be protected from 'buffoons' like Zuma. Dream on, I say. The American people directly elected George Bush into the presidency – not once, but twice. And now that Zuma might be president we are implored to begin the process of digging up – literally and figuratively – who killed who in the struggle. And where, if I may ask, would we stop with this? Would we be able to stop the recriminations and counter-recriminations? But what is it about Jacob Zuma that makes otherwise reasonable people lose all manner of proportion?

Some of my colleagues have tried to explain the intense dislike for Jacob Zuma in terms of race or class or gender. Those are only partial answers. Zuma is ultimately the victim of the cultural aesthetic of a non-racial, liberal modernity. This is the world which the writers and readers of this newspaper cohabit. But the majority of people in this country live outside this aesthetic. And they have the right to vote, *nogal*. That is what is driving everybody nuts in our fraternity. The 'great unwashed' are taking away the liberal modernist prerogative to govern.

Some years ago I suggested the following: 'Given their tolerance and inclusivity black people may turn out to be the true guardians of a properly contextualized and progressive liberalism ... that way John Rawls gets to meet Steve Biko.' As the traditional guardians of liberalism abandon some of its most venerable precepts, particularly the idea of innocent until proven guilty, we all need to step up to the plate and bring discussions of the rule of law to our communities. Jacob Zuma has been the test of whether the cultural aesthetic of a non-racial, liberal modernity can be sufficiently accommodating of the rights of those whose worldview we find objectionable.

As an epilogue it may be worth saying something about the changing fortunes of black intellectuals in the media throughout this saga. Throughout the Mbeki years some of us were celebrated as the best intellectuals in town. The praise came from both the black and white communities. I am not by any stretch of imagination suggesting there was universal acclaim. Thabo Mbeki's supporters hated our guts, and they let that be known in numerous columns and letters to the editor and through the president's own poisonous pen. Our fortunes rose in the media and among the chattering classes as it became apparent that the emperor had no clothes. Unfortunately, though, our opposition to Mbeki's racial nativism was taken to mean racial denialism on our part. And so when we turned the gaze to the problems of racism in the media, we in turn became the enemy within. Sipho Seepe captured these changing fortunes of black intellectuals: 'Blacks whose views coincide with those held by a majority of whites are said to be independent. Condemnation awaits those who dare to display any intellectual agency outside the script. Wits University hounded Prof Malegapuru Makgoba for daring to introduce the topic of Africanisation. Prof Mahmood Mamdani received a similar treatment at the University of Cape Town. Wits subsequently apologised.'[18]

18　Sipho Seepe, 'Black man stating his opinion risks losing approval of whites', *Business Day*, 6 May 2009.

Seepe reminded readers that our role as public intellectuals was to speak truth to both the black and the white establishment: 'in the same way that we took exception to racial reasoning in the black community, we should take a stand against what seems to be racial and supremacist reasoning in the white community. We should do so even if we risk being labelled "previously sensible."'

Seepe's article was soon followed by a letter in the *Business Day* from the CEO of the Institute of Race Relations, John Kane-Berman, dissociating the Institute from Seepe's writings:

> Views expressed by Prof. Sipho Seepe in a series of columns in *Business Day* (most recently on May 6, 'Black man stating his opinion risks losing approval of whites') may have been assumed to be those of the South African Institute of Race Relations. Although Seepe is its president, many of his views are not those of the Institute, which remains as strongly committed to the independence of the judiciary and the rule of law as it always has been.[19]

Running parallel with this disavowal of 'previously sensible' black intellectuals was a new focus on their academic credentials. Inspired by the Wits University Vice-Chancellor, Loyiso Nongxa, the line of attack was that we were mere commentators, not real intellectuals. The main argument was that real intellectuals need to have a record of publishing in academic journals and be rated by the National Research Foundation. This line of attack displayed shocking ignorance of the intellectual function. While the academic expert focuses on things practical, the intellectual is concerned with the moral dimension of things. While academics are bound by their professional disciplines, the intellectual answers to a higher calling of consciousness. It is precisely because of their semi-clerical and political heritage that intellectuals entered the public domain, with

19 John Kane-Berman, Letter to the Editor, *Business Day*, 8 May 2009.

the primary purpose of engaging with the moral implications of ideas. Their commitments are primarily moral and philosophical, not practical and instrumental. Thus, when Robert Oppenheimer developed the atomic bomb he was acting as an academic expert. It was only when he stepped into the public domain to talk not about the science of the bomb but about its morality that he became an intellectual.

Perhaps the best distinction between academic experts and intellectuals is provided by Richard Hofstadter. In his view the expert's essence is practicality and instrumentality of ideas; but practicality is not the essence of the intellectual's interest in ideas. As Ali Mazrui put it in Thandika Mkandawire's beautiful collection, *African Intellectuals*: 'an intellectual is anyone who pursues ideas qua ideas.' Academic expertise matters only to the extent that it strengthens an individual's arguments in the public domain. Academic expertise is therefore best seen as a prop, not as the essence of the intellectual. If academic expertise is a requirement of the intellectual function, then neither Studs Terkel nor Saul Alinsky nor Walter Sisulu nor Steve Biko would qualify as public intellectuals who, in the words of Garry Wills, 'engage citizens in philosophical self-examination at public meeting places'.[20]

Conclusion: the limits of liberal modernity

Some years ago I suggested that it may well be that the project of liberalism in South Africa suffers from its association with whiteness or, better put, with its inability to find comfort in an African cultural landscape. I suspected then that the historical context within which South African liberalism evolved prevented it from avoiding what Ira Katznelson called liberalism's indifference to the suffering of others.[21] The strange irony of the preceding story is that it is 'liberals'

20 Garry Wills, *Certain Trumpets: The Nature of Leadership* (New York: Simon & Schuster, 1995)
21 Ira Katznelson, *Liberalism's Crooked Circle* (Princeton, NJ: Princeton University Press, 1996).

who have shown an inability to appreciate what Isaiah Berlin called the irreducibility of cultural and political difference.

This is not a problem restricted to white people. I suspect that Thabo Mbeki suffered from liberal modernity's indifference to the voices of others. Thus the problem of dying babies in Frere Hospital in East London could not be as bad as everyone made it out to be because the national statistics told a different story. Was it not Mbeki's cabinet ministers Steve Tshwete and Penuell Maduna who went to a street corner, stood for a few seconds and then asked if anyone had been raped in that time? This stunt was meant to debunk the argument that women were being raped every other second in South Africa. Though the stunt may have been clever, it was in bad taste and showed lack of empathy for people's real life experiences.

Liberal cultural supremacy – of both the black and white kind – has alienated the great mass of people who exist outside its cultural boundaries. These are the people who turned out in huge droves to acclaim Jacob Zuma as the symbol of their cultural insurgency. Sex, Mr Steinberg, had nothing to do with it.

Mine is not an argument for cultural relativism but rather for cultural pluralism. Cultural relativism maintains that how people live their lives and treat each other is none of our business. Surely no democratic society can be built on such foundations. This is why we need to do everything we can to make sure we have a criminal justice system that works. If Jacob Zuma had been convicted of rape or the national director of public prosecutions had broken the law in dropping the charges against him, then no amount of cultural relativism would protect Zuma.

Cultural pluralism teaches something different: that our cultural values are not the only ones that matter in the world, that there is, in Walter Lippmann's formulation, a distinction between our universe and the universe, and that any assumption to the contrary is the first step towards tyranny. Moreover, tyranny can come in many forms, as much from the politicians as from civil society and the media. Cultural pluralism teaches us that the fact of his difference – from the social and cultural elite – does not disqualify Zuma from public office, especially if the majority of the people want him as their president. What would disqualify him would be when those cultural values are in conflict with the foundational values and principles of our constitutional democracy. As Robert Weisberg put it, in a democracy 'unadulterated tolerance is a dangerous illusion'.[22] As we navigate the invisible boundary between culture and politics we should take to heart the distinguished scholar Michael Walzer's argument that a pluralistic society is more likely to succeed by accommodating than by opposing the multiple identities of the men and women it aims to engage. 'Its aim, after all, is not full-time [cultural] conversion but political socialization [in the principles of democracy].'[23] Living with and being led by those whom history has taught us to despise may be a hard pill to swallow. But then again it is not called democracy for nothing.

22 Robert Weissberg, *Political Tolerance* (Thousand Oaks, CA: Sage Publications, 1998), 78.
23 Michael Walzer, *On Toleration* (New Haven: Yale University Press, 1997), 80.

5

Congress of the what? Prospects for opposition politics

Prior to the Polokwane conference, one of the often-repeated questions I was asked as a political commentator was whether the left was about to split off from the ANC. No matter how many times I said it would not happen soon, the question kept coming back. At some point I thought it was not so much a question as a wish. On the other hand the question I was never asked was when the 'right' would break from the ANC. It was only after Mbeki's defeat at Polokwane that this question began to be posed. The answer was of course the Congress of the People (Cope), which was led by some of Thabo Mbeki's closest allies: the former ANC chairperson Mosiuoa Lekota, the former Gauteng premier Mbhazima Shilowa and the former deputy minister of defence Mluleki George. The former deputy president and wife of Bulelani Ngcuka, Phumzile Mlambo-Ngcuka, and the businessman Saki Macozoma joined later.

To this day Mbeki has never come out publicly to say that he belonged or belongs to Cope, not even during the April 2009 election campaign. But when asked how he had voted, Mbeki protested that his vote was his secret. True enough, but it sounded rather odd coming from someone who had spent his whole life in the ANC and publicly campaigned for it while its leader; and now was rather coy about sharing with the public where his loyalties might lie.

The idea that Mbeki could be suspected of leaving the ANC to join a rival party was unthinkable for another reason. Listen to Mbeki describing how Oliver Tambo (O.R.) bequeathed this great organisation personally to him:

> As I have said, I visited O.R. in London in 1989 as he was recuperating from his stroke. On this occasion we discussed that our movement was faced with conducting our struggle in new and complex circumstances. He then communicated another mission, the most challenging since I first met him in Dar-es-Salaam 27 years earlier: look after the ANC and make sure we succeed. You will know what needs to be done.

And then:

> On O.R.'s instruction, in 1989, I began talking to Madiba, Nelson Mandela, by phone, while he was in prison. We continued this telephone contact after he was released in 1990, before I returned home. I must presume that O.R. authorized this contact to ensure that because of his guidance that his lifelong friend and comrade, Madiba, would provide, I would not make mistakes that would compromise the advance of our struggle and revolution.

And then again, rather self-consciously: 'It might appear to the casual reader of this contribution to this book of tribute to Oliver Tambo, on what would have been his 90th birthday, that this humble piece is more about myself rather than the immortal hero of our struggle, Oliver Reginald Tambo.'[1]

1 Thabo Mbeki, 'A great giant who strode the globe like a colossus', in Z. Pallo Jordan (ed.), *Oliver Tambo Remembered* (Johannesburg: Macmillan, 2007), xviii.

Each of these passages contains important giveaway lines: 'look after the ANC ... you will know what needs to be done'; 'I must presume that O.R. authorized ...'; 'it might appear ... that this piece is more about myself'. It was just this sense of personal authorisation that informed Mbeki's view of authority. He, and he alone, had received the historical mandate from Oliver Tambo. It was this sense of authorisation that put on him the burden of choosing the next leader, Mbeki's successor. As far as he was concerned, that person was certainly not Jacob Zuma.

The first public suggestion that a new party might be in the offing came when Mosiuoa Lekota announced on Radio 702 in September 2008 that he was serving divorce papers on the party he had led as chairperson over the previous ten years. The grounds for the divorce were that the newly elected leadership had abandoned the values of the ANC. Lekota announced that a national convention would be held to determine whether a new party should be formed. Heeding his call, five thousand people converged on the Sandton Convention Centre to participate in and witness the formation of the new party. This gathering was to prepare for the formal launch of the party in Bloemfontein in December 2008. The keynote address was given by one of the founder-members of the black consciousness movement and principal of the University of South Africa, Barney Pityana.

On the eve of the Bloemfontein launch the ANC went to court to challenge the new party's right to use the name of Congress of the People, maintaining that it was the property of the ANC, because the ANC had organised the historic congress of the same name in 1955 in Kliptown, where its guiding document, the Freedom Charter, was adopted. As a black consciousness activist in the 1980s, I spent countless hours and endless nights arguing with ANC activists about the historic Congress of the People and the Freedom Charter. Our view was that the ANC's multi-racial alliance as well as its claim in the Freedom Charter that the land belonged to all was a falsification of history. We rejected the Kliptown Congress of the People as a 'soporific'[2] (to use Steve Biko's word) which created the false impression that progress was being made in race relations in South Africa. At that time ANC leaders vehemently defended their history. Now those very same people were arguing against the ANC's claims to that very same history.

The court case notwithstanding, Cope soon got off the ground. Its eyes were firmly set on the Eastern Cape where Mbeki had received the strongest backing. A number of senior Mbeki allies in the province announced that they were leaving the ANC, among them Nosimo Balindlela and several members of the Eastern Cape legislature. Later, Cope's election head, Mlungisi Hlongwane, returned to the ANC fold, charging that the new party was driven by a Xhosa agenda. Cope was launched to even greater fanfare in Bloemfontein on 16 December 2008, a date chosen for its association with the launch of the ANC in that city in 1912. Cope was so confident about its prospects that some of its leaders predicted it would get over 50 per cent of the vote in the forthcoming general election in April 2009. The logic, I suppose, was that the support Mbeki received at Polokwane would be reflected in the general population. Cope's leaders were convinced that South Africans would be put off by Jacob Zuma because of the controversies around him – hence Lekota's constant attacks on Zuma for his rape and corruption charges. Cope was also of the belief that the majority of the population would be repelled by the language of Julius Malema. Even though I was also put off by Malema, I was not convinced that Cope would present us with a substantively different politics.[3]

Why am I saddened by the breaking up of the African National Congress (ANC)? After all, I have never been a member of the organisation. On

2 Steve Biko, *I Write What I Like* (Johannesburg: Picador, 2004), 23.
3 Xolela Mangcu, 'Visionless rival to ANC could turn to nightmare', *Business Day*, 16 October 2008.

the contrary, I have often been at odds with some of its philosophical positions.

I have over the past decade also been critical of its public policy positions – from HIV/AIDS to economics. I have argued that we need a vibrant opposition that would keep the ANC on its toes. Our experience with HIV/AIDS, and Zimbabwe's experience with Zanu (PF), point to the dangers of dominant parties with no viable opposition.

So why should I feel sad instead of celebrating the new party as the fulfilment of that ideal? My sadness has to do with a distinction I make between procedural democracy and substantive democracy. Procedural democracy is the skeleton that makes up the body politic, and substantive democracy is the lifeblood of the body politic.

It may well be that the arrival of a new party contributes to procedural plurality but does not automatically translate into a substantively democratic culture. In fact, political plurality can easily be either wonderfully democratic or terribly anarchic. To avoid the latter, plurality requires at least two things: vision and leadership.

Vision requires that there should be a common set of values among people in a movement even as they have reasonable differences about strategies and tactics for pursuing those values. The question is whether the new party is driven by a set of common values.

I have no doubt that there are many people in the new movement who are motivated by their unhappiness with the vulgarity of certain members of the new ANC. It would be foolish for the new leaders to dismiss those people as enemies who ought to be punished and expelled.

But it is also clear that for many in the new movement this is a fight back by those who were dislodged at Polokwane. These are the people who are likely to turn the dream of plurality into a nightmare of anarchy as they fight for positions.

The absence of a set of values could see the new party turning in on itself. The problem is that once a process is set in motion – in the absence of common orienting values – there is no way of putting the genie back into the bottle.

In addition to the bun fights for positions and patronage, there is the all-important question of leadership. I am just not sure that having known Mbeki-ites such as Mosiuoa Lekota and Mluleki George does anything to dispel the idea that this is another bunch of disgruntled individuals ready to abandon an entire heritage because they lost out in a leadership race. A sensible voter could not be blamed for asking: were they not part of the team that created the mess in the first place?

And this is not about ideology. How different would the policies of the new party be from the centre-left policies of the ANC or the centre-right policies of the Democratic Alliance?

The truth is that this is a man-made disaster. Under a different leadership the whole circus could have been averted. I can imagine that Nelson Mandela's heart is bleeding at seeing the party to which he gave his entire being going up in smoke. I can imagine many ANC people feel that way.

Some analysts point to the crowds that fill the venues when the new leaders speak. But how many of those people have been with the ANC in exile or underground or as it shepherded society through our transition, losing people such as Chris Hani in the process?

Cope's teething problems: the men who would be kings

One of my biggest mistakes as a political commentator was a suggestion I made that the ANC ought to look to Mosiuoa Lekota as a successor to Mbeki. The argument was motivated by the following reasoning. For fifteen years the ANC had been run by individuals and factions that had spent the better part of their lives either in prison (as with Nelson Mandela) or in exile (as with Thabo Mbeki). While Mandela did a brilliant job in bringing us back from the precipice of racial conflagration and while Mbeki did his bit in trumpeting transformation, neither had experience of the mass democratic movement. South Africa, it seemed to me, needed a leader who would steer it away from Mbeki's racial nativism and the authoritarian leadership characteristic of the ANC's exile culture.

I was warned by many in the ANC that I did not understand their organisation or Lekota. Apparently Lekota had ensconced himself in the bosom of Mbeki's power network. Even when I touted his name, I expressed concern about his abrasive style but thought that was something that could be worked on. What I ignored was Richard Neustadt's injunction that by the time they run for office, presidents are fully formed individuals; their temperament is unlikely to change.[4] Lekota approached politics like a street fighter: brash, abrasive and outright rude. Once in a radio interview with John Perlman he called me a 'young man' who did not understand the ANC. Those were the days when he was still defending the ANC. On another occasion he defended the government's arms deal by telling critics that the government had made its decision and no one could do anything about it. On yet another occasion he said that Zuma's followers were not well in their heads: *ababhadlanga*.

I asked him about this statement at a conference of opposition parties hosted by Radio 702 in Sandton. Lekota had been going on about how rude Julius Malema and the new group of ANC leaders were. So I rose to remind him of his own language in respect of Zuma's followers. He denied ever saying such a thing. The show's hostess, Redi Direko, reminded him where, when and what he had said. Lekota insisted that he had not used the word *izibhanxa*, which is the word I incorrectly attributed to him. He had said '*ababhadlanga*'. I pointed out that he was splitting hairs: the words are almost interchangeable in isiXhosa. It's like making a distinction between an idiot and a fool. He could have used *izibhanxa* and the effect would have been the

---

4 Matthew J. Dickinson and Elizabeth A. Neustadt (eds.), *Guardian of the Presidency: The Legacy of Richard E. Neustadt* (Washington: Brookings Institution Press, 2007), 67.

same. That's when Lekota lost it. He wagged his finger and instructed me to 'sit down, sit down, sit down!' I reminded Lekota that he was no longer the chairman of the ruling party and was not at liberty to order people around at a press conference. I don't think I have ever seen the man so angry, at least not in public.

But I was not the only one who found Lekota insufferable. His new party seems to have thought so when they went outside to find a more attractive candidate as leader. The ensuing internal leadership battles did not inspire confidence. Those who saw Lekota's brash personality as a liability in the elections looked to Shilowa as their alternative. Apparently Shilowa was also closer to the money men behind Cope, many of whom had made their money through black economic empowerment programmes. Shilowa's wife, Wendy Luhabe, was arguably the leading woman beneficiary of BEE in the country.

In a bid to resolve the leadership contest, the party first decided that there would be no election for leader at its founding conference in Bloemfontein. Instead, the triumvirate of Lekota as president with Mbhazima Shilowa and Lynda Odendaal as deputy presidents was simply presented as a fait accompli. But this did not quell the leadership squabbles, and Cope finally brought in a completely new, fresh face and political outsider, the respected cleric Bishop Mvume Dandala. I was one of those who initially thought this was an inspired appointment that would constitute a real challenge to the ANC. When the political analyst Mcebisi Ndletyana called to say Cope would announce Dandala as its leader, I simply gasped: 'Wow.' In one of my columns I described Dandala's selection as an inspired move.

his elevation to the leadership of Cope puts me in somewhat of a quandary. I trust the man, but distrust his party. And so I would like to ask him to help me navigate that fine line. First, he would have to dispel any suspicion that he is a front for those who lost with Thabo

Mbeki at Polokwane. Given the circumstances of Cope's birth, that is going to be a tall order – even for a man of the cloth. But if he successfully disabuses the nation of those suspicions, then he might be headed for the Union Buildings in 2014. If he fails he would have diminished himself in the eyes of so many of us who hold him in love and reverence. So there you go, Mfundisi (Reverend), may all the blessings you have accumulated over the years protect you from the rough and tumble of politics, and from this sometimes acerbic pen.[5]

It did not take very long for me to realise that my personal affection for the man had blinded me to his political weakness. If Lekota behaved like a bully, Dandala was too much of a sweetheart. He was not the kind to rouse the masses, a quality one would need in putting up a fight against a formidable competitor like Zuma. For instance, Dandala's decision not to criticise Zuma during the election campaign struck me as rather strange. The decision to appoint Dandala also irked those who felt he had been parachuted into the position of leader from out of the blue. The party's second deputy president, Lynda Odendaal, apparently asked him to step down shortly after he was brought in. Rumour also has it that the money men in Cope were the instigators of the approach to Dandala in an attempt to abort Lekota's presidential ambitions. At one point Lekota dissociated himself from Mbeki's legacy and was thus regarded as not entirely dependable. It did not help matters that shortly before the campaign Lekota announced that the election posters and the ballot paper would carry his face instead of Dandala's. The problems seemed to pile on just as the elections were getting closer. Cope's election campaign was a shambles, with rumours abounding that some communications experts were disgruntled because they had not been paid. On the streets there was hardly any Cope poster in sight until very late in the day. By that time the ANC had covered almost

5 'Dandala is a great choice as the face of Cope', *The Weekender*, 21–22 February 2009.

every lamp-post with Jacob Zuma's picture. Cope thus entered the election without a clear message about who was ultimately in charge, Lekota or Dandala.

At the root of Cope's problems lay the popular perception that the new party was a disgruntled movement led by people who had lost out in the ANC leadership campaign. It did not help that Mbeki stayed away from the important ANC National Executive Committee meeting immediately after the Polokwane conference at which the party's programme for the following year would be presented. In fact Cope's leadership underestimated Mbeki's unpopularity not only within the ANC but among the general population. And so from the start I never gave Cope much of a chance in the 2009 general election. In fact, I predicted that the new kid on the block would be lucky to breach the 10 per cent voting barrier.[6]

There is only one reason the Congress of the People (Cope) was trounced by the African National Congress (ANC) in the by-elections in Port Elizabeth: people are not stupid.

There is also one reason Cope is going to be trounced by the ANC in the general elections next month: people are not stupid.

You cannot parade a group of Thabo Mbeki supporters in front of people and expect them to believe it is something else.

Take a look at the Cope list: Nosimo Balindlela, she who was just kicked out by the ANC in the Eastern Cape; Smuts Ngonyama, the enforcer in Mbeki's presidency; Phumzile Mlambo-Ngcuka, once Mbeki's favourite for the presidency.

The man I pity in all of this is Mvume Dandala. Try as he might to distance himself from Mbeki, the mere suspicion of Mbeki's hand in all of this is enough to turn people away. If anything, that is the measure of the man's unpopularity in this country. He remains the albatross around Cope's neck.

6 Xolela Mangcu, 'Cope does not stand a chance in elections', *The Weekender*, 7 March 2009.

I laughed listening to Cope supporters – chief among them the SABC – explaining away the party's loss. The broadcaster insisted that this was no indication of what will happen at the general election. They brought in an analyst who reckoned that Cope had done extremely well for a new party. Apparently Cope had taken a significant section of ANC support – which leaves you wondering why the support matters if it cannot give you a single ward.

Prior to the elections all one heard was that the Eastern Cape was Cope's heartland. Talk about a significant downward revision of expectations – after the fact.

But imagine if Cope had won in Port Elizabeth. I can assure you the language would have been different. But then politics is a world of spin, which would make a bishop's task doubly difficult.

The biggest downward revision is going to come from Cope's projected 51% (or Saki Macozoma's 30%) for the general elections to something below 10%. I suggest Cope revise the expectations now lest they have to somersault later.

I am not a gambler, but I like bets when it comes to these things. In a bet no one can turn around and offer an excuse – they must just cough up and buy me that bottle of King George.

It does not help that Mosiuoa Lekota and the rest of the leadership speak as if they are from Mars and Venus. A section of the Cope leadership believes in affirmative action and BEE, but Lekota likens the programmes to apartheid. Talk about a warped sense of history. And what is so difficult about speaking with one clear voice on HIV/AIDS? You could really be forgiven for thinking the leaders belong to different parties.

Cope tells us that Dandala will be its presidential candidate, but Lekota's face will be on the ballot. I can imagine the confusion among those who will go out to vote for the bishop and then can't find him on the ballot. Given our penchant for mood swings, they might just turn to the next familiar face on the ballot – Jacob Zuma.

And you ask yourself why a new party should be so feckless a mere six weeks from an election.

The ANC's show of strength

Mbeki probably did himself a favour by not attending the ANC's NEC meeting just after Polokwane. It was the biggest show of strength the new leadership of the ANC had put together till then. The ANC reconfigured its campaign: instead of fighting the new party, the ANC decided to show its strength instead. The first such show of strength was the rally for Jacob Zuma's announcement of the ANC's 8 January statement in East London. The aim was to take the fight (politically) to the Eastern Cape, where the ANC had trounced Cope in a series of recent by-elections. The Eastern Cape was not only the biggest province in the country but was also the heartland of the ANC. By bringing 80,000 people to a jam-packed stadium the ANC sent out a clear message to Cope: 'not in my backyard'. The rally was broadcast countrywide on the evening news, sending shivers down the spine of many a Cope follower. There were rumours that the ANC had bused in people from other parts of the country. Be that as it may, the rally took the wind out of the sails of Cope's campaign.

But the real show of strength was still coming: at the party's Siyanqoba rally in Johannesburg on 19 April 2009, held in the gigantic Ellis Park and Johannesburg stadiums. (Such is the state of democratic competition in South Africa that the dominant party celebrates before the election takes place.) I thought I should attend the event if only to witness for myself the 'Zuma mania' that was then gripping the country. I was in the company of people with connections in the ANC and so we were quickly spirited off to a private suite where we could have breakfast shielded from the sweltering heat. I whispered to a friend that the ANC risked embarrassing itself by hiring such a big stadium. But as early morning gave way to mid-morning, the rows of empty red seats were replaced by the sight of endless yellow T-shirts. The crowd, which had now swelled to capacity, broke into a thunderous roar when Nelson Mandela made his appearance. This was a major coup for Zuma. In the previous weeks there were rumours that the ANC had taken the ailing Nelson Mandela against his wishes to a rally in Idutywa. At Idutywa and in subsequent interviews with the press, Zuma sought to assure the nation that Madiba had in fact requested to be taken to the rally. But this did not convince the critics. Madiba's reappearance in Ellis Park was thus meant not only to prove the critics wrong but also to give an additional shot in the arm to the ANC's campaign behind Zuma.

Outside the Ellis Park stadium in Johannesburg thousands of people struggled to gain entrance. And then one of the display screens showed the neighbouring Johannesburg Stadium also filled to capacity. One stadium I could understand, but two stadiums in close proximity to each other? In short there were close to 200,000 people massed together who had come to hear Zuma.

The event confirmed much of what I had been saying in my columns: that there was a world out there beyond the ken of the chattering classes. In Johannesburg this world converged in celebration and indeed affirmation of one of the most reviled political figures in the mainstream news media. How could an individual whom we in the media viewed as morally transgressive be the object of so much attention and affection from so many people? Did this mean that the people themselves were morally transgressive or suffered from an acute case of false consciousness? And how could the revered Nelson Mandela repeatedly come out in support of this deeply flawed politician?

Zuma gave a long speech that the crowd hardly listened to. It was when he belted out his 'Umshini wam' and broke into his signature dance that the crowd literally went into a frenzy. To those of us who came of political age in the consciousness-raising 1970s and 1980s, this was rather bizarre. Zuma's politics all too easily seemed to be about spectacle and no message. The very content of politics had been transformed from Thabo Mbeki's sonorous speeches peppered with references to W.B. Yeats and John Donne into a ritual of mass collective identification. Not only had the profile of the leader changed but also that of the follower. There was something frightening about so many people in awe of one individual leader.

It is at such moments of euphoria that the intellectual should guard against being completely absorbed in the mass adulation. No individual leader, Zuma included, is free of the foibles of human nature and can resist the historical tendency for politics to turn good men into bad (and it has been mostly men). And yet the independent intellectual does not live outside society and thus has the capacity to be moved by collective celebration. In C. Wright Mills's formulation, the activist intellectual is the one who simultaneously educates and receives education from struggling people in society. As someone who started out quite critical of Zuma, I found myself gradually being educated by the debates surrounding him, whether it was because of the sense of injustice and unfairness I sensed or because my childhood friends in Ginsberg kept telling me that I was out of touch with their realities. The more I listened to these inner and external voices, the more it became obvious to me that Jacob Zuma challenged some of the most deeply held and cherished cultural assumptions of the modernist elite, that he had become a sociological lightning rod for a deeply traditional but also marginalised section of our society. And this section could be marginalised in every way but one, their constitutionally protected right to vote. This was the only way that they were going to make their voices heard: at the ballot box.

The 2009 elections and identity politics

The 2009 elections were probably the most hotly contested since the first democratic elections in 1994. They were also different from prior elections because of the participation of the Congress of the

People, a party that emerged from within the bosom of the ANC. The question on everyone's mind was whether its emergence would move the country away from racial voting and inaugurate a non-racial electoral pattern. The literature on elections in multi-ethnic societies is often characterised by a debate between those who, following David Horowitz, argue that elections constitute an ethnic-racial census and those who insist that people vote on the basis of retrospective evaluations of party performance.[7]

There has been some debate about whether South Africa's voters have fallen on one side or other of this divide. I am one of those who would argue that the idea of a racial census still best describes voting patterns since 1994. In 1994 the ANC won 62.65 per cent of the national vote, with 75 per cent of that support coming from the African community. In 1999 the party increased its share of the vote to 66.35 per cent and in 2004 to 69.69 per cent.

Opposition politics were just as determined by racial solidarity. In the 1999 elections the Democratic Party, the predecessor of the Democratic Alliance, used a strategy of racial mobilisation to oust the New National Party (NNP) as the official opposition. The Democratic Party's 'Fight back' campaign was widely interpreted as a rallying cry for whites to band together to protect their interests. The party's leader, Tony Leon, was never coy about exploiting the *gatvol* factor among 'ethnic minorities'. He would no doubt worry about attracting black voters only once he had secured his electoral base among whites. Leon's gamble worked, and in 1999 the Democratic Party became the new official opposition by offering a more muscular alternative to the NNP, which was painted as having sold out the white community by going into bed with the ANC in the first post-1994 government. As a result of this strategy of racial mobilisation, the newly reconstituted Democratic Party increased its share of the vote from 1.73 per

---

7 D.A. Horowitz, *Ethnic Groups in Conflict* (Berkeley: University of California, 1985) and Pippa Norris and Robert Mattes, 'Does ethnicity determine support for the governing party', John F. Kennedy School of Government, Harvard University, 2003.

cent in 1994 to 9.56 per cent in 1999.

At the time Steven Friedman noted that 'these elections may even provide some evidence for claims that divided societies offer rewards to ethnic outbidders – that is, those able to present themselves as more plausible vehicles of ethnic confrontation than their rivals'.[8] As if to prove Friedman's argument, the Democratic Alliance increased its share of the national vote to 12.3 per cent in 2004 and 16.66 per cent in 2009.

In a *Business Day* column, Tony Leon, the former leader of the Democratic Alliance (DA), likened the loyalty of ANC supporters to that reserved by football fans for their teams: 'Like the venerable English team [Manchester United], it matters little that the long-serving captain was dropped (recalled) just months ago, or that the team itself had, in key areas, performed indifferently. Even the emergence from within its ranks of a breakaway team barely affected the overall result. The brand loyalty and the powerful sense of self-identity, wrapped up in voting for it, powered the ANC to an emphatic victory.'[9]

Leon described the 'gulf' between the ANC and its nearest rival, the DA, as 'ethnic'. However, it is a combination of race and history that came to define the battle between Cope and the ANC, hence the fight over names and symbols between the two parties. Where Cope succeeded was the way it redefined the landscape of opposition politics. The massacre of the opposition parties in the 2009 elections most likely had to do with Cope's emergence. The new party attracted supporters mainly from the United Democratic Movement in the Eastern Cape, and from the Independent Democrats in the Western Cape and the Northern Cape. Cope must have been disappointed by the fact that the ANC obtained 69 per cent of the vote in the

8 Steven Friedman, *Journal of Democracy*, 10, 4 (1999), 3–18..
9 Tony Leon, 'Big winners, big losers: an epic end to poetic campaign', *Business Day*, 28 April 2009.

much-coveted Eastern Cape. It would also no doubt have won over members from the ANC nationally. But in the end Cope failed to convince enough ANC supporters that it was the real custodian of ANC history or enough DA supporters that it was the real non-racial alternative to the ANC.

This is not to say the existence of Cope is insignificant, just as the existence of the DA is not insignificant. The presence of another group of thirty MPs should lead to more vibrant parliamentary debates, even though it will not do much to change the dynamics of power fundamentally. An ANC stalwart once jokingly said to me that even though the ANC did not win a two-thirds majority in 2009, it could always rely on the lone member of the Azanian People's Organisation to reach that threshold.

Whither opposition politics?

The real question is whether Cope will do better in the next general elections or whether it will be eviscerated like the other smaller parties in 2009. I personally see no further growth in Cope, if only because many of the people who supported it genuinely believed that the ANC was on its knees. Those who put money into it must have thought that the party would capture state power and thus maintain their access to state resources. Though this did not happen, the party will still have ample resources through private sector funding. Its leading members belong to Elephant Consortium, which stood to gain millions of rands from the planned sale of shares in Vodacom by Telkom, in which it owned a stake, to the UK-based Vodafone. Apparently some Cope leaders had even borrowed money to finance Cope's campaign in anticipation of the payout. The *Mail & Guardian* identified senior Cope leaders and backers identified with the consortium as Smuts Ngonyama, Gloria Serobe and Wendy Luhabe, while the former director-general of the Department of Communications and now a senior Cope leader, Lyndall Mafole-Shope, is said to have played an important role in government's approval of the listing. The Independent Communications Authority and Cosatu approached the North Gauteng High Court for an interdict against the sale on the ground of insufficient public consultation. However, the court rejected their application because of the financial implications for the companies and for the country.[10] Although the deal was vehemently opposed by Jacob Zuma, many people in the ANC were shocked when President Kgalema Motlanthe approved the deal in cabinet. Motlanthe's decision may still haunt the ANC when it has to contend with Cope's war chest in future elections.

On the day the 2009 election results were announced, the leader of the Independent Democrats called for a coalition of opposition parties, a call that had been made prior to the elections by Helen Zille and would be repeated later by Mbhazima Shilowa after the election. In an article in the *Sunday Times*, Shilowa noted that it was 'a matter of historical cause that opposition parties fared badly, with the exception of the DA and Cope'. Shilowa argued that a coalition of opposition parties could be 'the tonic the country needs to reshape our opposition politics and give South Africans an alternative voice with the capacity to become the next government'.[11] What Shilowa said in the article contradicts his rejection of alliances in an interview with the political scientist Susan Booysen prior to the election. In that interview Shilowa categorically stated that 'alliances at this point in time are out of the question, but we will cooperate with others on specific issues ... Cope will not go into a coalition which it does not lead, where its identity will be subsumed by others.'[12] Shilowa's insistence on a leading role for his party points to a general problem

10 Lloyd Gedye and Matuma Letsoalo, 'Vodacom: ANC's elephant hunt', *Mail & Guardian*, 15 May 2009.
11 Mbhazima Shilowa, 'Now is the time for a united opposition', *Sunday Times*, 26 July 2009.
12 Susan Booysen, 'Congress of the People: between foothold of hope and slippery slope' in Roger Southall and John Daniel (eds.), *Zunami: The 2009 South African Elections* (Johannesburg: Jacana Media, 2009), 112.

with coalition politics in general. Each party brings not only its own ambitions but also its discordant voices into the coalition.

Booysen is rather sanguine about Cope's performance in the 2009 elections. She points to the fact that Cope obtained 7.4 per cent of the vote in a short space of time, and that it became the official opposition in several provinces. She reckons that most of its support came not from former supporters of opposition parties but from former supporters of the ANC. It is not exactly clear on what basis this conclusion is reached other than a conversation with an official from the CSIR. The effect of the claim is to obscure the fact that Cope fell far short of what its leaders had expected would happen and the disappointment that came in its wake. Put differently, if Cope's leaders had had a clear crystal ball that showed them the election outcome, they never would have left the ANC. The reality is that whether Cope took its support from the ANC or from the opposition, the gap between the ANC and the opposition parties remains unchanged.

Except for the Western Cape, where the ruling party lost, the ANC remains by far the dominant force in South African politics fifteen years into our democracy. Anthony Butler writes that on a negative reading the ANC lost anywhere between 5 and 10 per cent of its vote between 2004 and 2009 but this was offset by its gains in KwaZulu-Natal.[13] This loss for the ANC can be interpreted as a major development but only on the assumption that the loss will continue inexorably. It may well be that many of the people who voted for Cope in the hope that it would do well may return to the ANC fold, leaving only diehard members behind. A great deal of this also depends on how Jacob Zuma and the ANC conduct themselves in office, not so much in terms of the much vaunted concept of service delivery but in reaching out to communities. The biggest complaint

13 Anthony Butler, 'The ANC's national election campaign of 2009: Siyanqoba' in Roger Southall and John Daniels (eds.), *Zunami*.

against Mbeki was not simply that people were not benefiting from the new dispensation but that he was a president who simply could not be bothered by their plight.

I am less sanguine about Cope's prospects, though. This may have much to do with the circumstances of its founding as a cynical means of Thabo Mbeki's disgruntled supporters to reposition themselves after having lost a democratic party election. It is possible that with time, and therefore some distance from Mbeki's routing at Polokwane, people will forget why Cope was formed and begin to vote for it on the basis of retrospective evaluations, particularly at the local level. This is hard to see now. Race and history and the power of incumbency will give the ANC the edge until an organic crisis produces a social movement that challenges the ANC on the basis of real issues instead of party manoeuvres. For now we can only hope for greater internal debates and struggles in the ANC. Steven Friedman captures the centrality of internal contestation in the ANC as follows:

Given the ANC's lopsided majority, its internal politics is likely to provide more important clues to the state of democracy than any contest between the government and the opposition, at least for the next five years. While the current leadership is in a stronger position to extend its hold over the movement, the outcome is not assured, and the 'internal opposition' should remain a factor that the leadership will be forced to acknowledge.[14]

The ANC's continued electoral dominance also means that South Africa's democracy needs to be strengthened in ways that go beyond electoral politics. Although political dominance does tend to go with a disproportionate influence over other state institutions – the president chooses who becomes chief justice or the chairperson of

14 S. Friedman, *Journal of Democracy*, 10, 4 (1999), 3–18.

the SABC board – a vibrant opposition can only be effective within the context of a credible media, judiciary, civil society and a strong party, which can all in different ways serve as checks and balances on the government. The challenge is to use this democratic moment to strengthen not only our electoral politics but our political culture, including the culture of those institutions.

In time, an opposition party will emerge not as a result of party political intrigues, which is how Cope came into being, but as an organic response to social crisis and in protest against a ruling party that is no longer able to speak with sufficient authority and legitimacy to the broad spectrum of a plural society. The question is whether the ANC will respond to that challenge creatively and tolerantly or with the militarism discussed in Chapter 2. As Ibbo Mandaza points out in his introduction to Edgar Tekere's autobiography, violence has often been the recourse of postcolonial governments facing an organic crisis and a rising tide of opposition. According to Mandaza, it is their technical and economic incapacity that leads governments to use violence as the preferred method of rule in postcolonial societies.[15] In the following chapter I explore whether Jacob Zuma will take the ANC in the direction of militarism or democratic tolerance.

15 Ibbo Mandaza, Introduction, *Edgar '2Boy' Zivanai Tekere: A Life Time of Struggle* (Harare: Sapes Books, 2007).

6

Making government responsive: historical, symbolic and institutional imagination

The importance of history in governance

In their book, *Thinking in Time*, American presidential analysts Richard Neustadt and Ernest May bring to the attention of policy-makers the profundity of what is often a taken-for-granted and even clichéd statement: that the past matters more than we care to admit in how we think about the present and the future.[1] Indeed, the future can come from nowhere but the past. The line from the past to the future is not necessarily a linear one: it often follows Immanuel Kant's dictum that 'out of the crooked timber of humanity nothing straight was ever made'.[2]

There are indeed as many cultures in the world as there are people. The great public debate of the past fifty years has been where the accent should lie: whether on universal values or on the plurality of social identities. Universalists or modernists argue that an emphasis on difference makes the creation of community impossible, while postmodernists and pluralists argue that universalism is suffocating and oppressive of other cultures. My own view has always been that

1 Ernest May and Richard Neustadt, *Thinking in Time: Uses of History for Decision Makers* (New York: Free Press, 1988).
2 Isaiah Berlin, *The Crooked Timber of Humanity* (London: John Murray, 1990).

the postmodern revolution was necessary if we were to repudiate the arrogant assumptions and certitudes that underpinned the age of 'Euromegalomania' (that's the great historian Eric Hobsbawm's formulation, not mine).[3] But such repudiation must take place, in the words of Isaiah Berlin, within 'the human horizon' in order to make intercommunicability possible: 'intercommunication between cultures in time and space is only possible because what makes men human is common to them, and acts as a bridge between them.'[4]

Neustadt and May started their book, *Thinking in Time*, with the concern that there were too many people who 'did not know any history to speak of and were unaware of suffering any lack, who thought the world was new and its problems fresh (all made since Hiroshima, Vietnam, Watergate or the last elections) and that decisions in the public realm only require reason or emotion, as preferred'. They closed their book with Thucydides' proposition that 'human nature remains constant – or better perhaps, that dilemmas of human governance remain so – in short that 2500 years ago bad and good political judgments were to be found in about the same proportion as today'.[5]

Over the past fifteen years my lament has been the pretence among our leaders that the world began in 1994 and that its problems were purely of a technical nature. The magic of that date is supposed to have separated us from all that went before it. We were all meant to check our prejudices at the gate; those who forgot to do so are mere aberrations, just 'bad apples' in a bag otherwise full of good apples. We fool ourselves of course. Much of our social behaviour travels with us across space and time. It is this lack of a sense of historical continuity that acts as an impediment to much of our political imagination. The lack of historical imagination extends to the black

3 Eric Hobsbawm quoted in Ira Katznelson, *Liberalism's Crooked Circle* (Princeton, NJ: Princeton University Press, 1996), 128.
4 Isaiah Berlin, *The Crooked Timber of Humanity*, 11.
5 Ernest May and Richard Neustadt, *Thinking in Time*, 265.

community as well. This may come as a surprise given all the talk about an African Renaissance. But the African Renaissance was more a cerebral movement in the minds of a few leaders than a historic shift in our collective imagination.

One of the great ironies about Mbeki is that, erudite as he was, he lacked a sense of history. This assertion will strike many as strange in view of Mbeki's erudition and passion for Africa's history. Suffice it to say, by a 'sense of history' I do not mean knowledge of history. Knowledge of history can be acquired through wide reading, travelling, conversation and so on. By a sense of history I mean a cultivated sensibility about community experiences – what has gone before and how we ought to avoid the mistakes of that past. Intellectually, Mbeki knew that to seek to extend power was a bad idea, but ultimately he did not have the temperament to live by that insight. This lack of history found its way into our public life and then into the way we were governed. We were no longer historical actors determining our futures but passive spectators in a game designed and played by technocrats.

How technocracy undermined historical imagination

In 1994 the ANC-led government announced the Reconstruction and Development Programme (RDP) as its blueprint for remaking South African society. The RDP had laudable goals such as the provision of housing and social services on a mass scale for the historically disadvantaged black population. I was out of the country at the time studying at Cornell University. My good friend, the author of *Black Athena*, Martin Bernal, once shared with me his interpretation of goings-on back home. Not only did he have a knowledge of history but a deep sense of it as well. Still ringing in my mind is a comment he made about our new beginnings: 'It's as if the ANC has gone back to the 1950s without making a stop in the 1970s.' What he was saying was that it is not enough to go back in history: it is also how you go back in history and the lessons you choose to select as you delve historically.

At the heart of the RDP was what James C. Scott has called high modernism. This is the idea that governments can reorder society with a certain mechanical precision backed by scientific and technical expertise. Scott calls it an illusion whose value for the bureaucrats lies in 'dismembering an exceptionally complex set of human relations and processes in order to isolate the single element of instrumental value'. For the modern state the 'single element of instrumental value' has been state revenue. This fixation with numbers has not changed very much over the past two centuries.[6]

The instrumentalist idea of society as malleable in the hands of suitably qualified experts is of course the defining feature of Enlightenment rationality and has informed public administration and planning for the past two centuries. Reacting to the social misery that came in the wake of the Industrial Revolution, the founder of the science of administration, Woodrow Wilson, remarked in horror: 'A new era has come upon us like a sudden vision of things unprophesied, and for which no polity has been prepared.'[7] The solution, Wilson counselled, was a science of administration that would straighten the workings of government and society. Thus public administrators and planners borrowed heavily from the emergent science of management developed by Frederick Taylor. In fact one of Taylor's best friends and collaborators, Harlow Person, played a crucial role in the conception of planning as a scientific enterprise. For Person the result of planning ought to be 'standard component objectives, standard facilities for producing them and standard modes of manipulation – all with standard qualities, standard quantities and standard timing'.[8] But as James Scott points out, the desire for standardisation was not a left-

6 James C. Scott, *Seeing like a State* (New Haven: Yale University Press, 1999), 21.
7 Woodrow Wilson, 'The science of administration', 1887.
8 Cited in Dwight Waldo, *The Administrative State: A Study of the Political Theory of American Public Administration* (New York: The Ronald Press Company, 1948), 403.

wing or right-wing project: 'high modernist faith was no respecter of traditional political boundaries; it could be found across the political spectrum, from left to right but particularly among those who wanted to use state power to bring about huge, utopian changes in work habits, living patterns, moral conduct, and worldview.'[9]

South Africa's RDP had all the characteristics of what Alan Mabin calls a 'left modernism' that dated back to the 1980s, and it reflected a profound lack of any sense of history. Without any policy ideas in place the ANC relied heavily on planners from the white universities, most of whom would have had little sense of black history. As I described in an earlier book, *Emerging Johannesburg*, this left-modernist idea represented a departure from the black consciousness themes of community self-reliance that Martin Bernal reminded me about at Cornell.

Much has been made of the fact that Mbeki undermined the RDP. But what Mbeki did was to replace the ANC's 'left-wing modernism' with a government-led right-wing economic modernism in the form of Gear (the Growth, Employment and Redistribution strategy). As with the RDP, the logic was that if you played around with certain technical economic variables, many of our social problems would be alleviated. The Gear strategy rested on a simple and simplistic syllogism: if you got the prices right (budget deficits, interest rates, wages), then the levels of foreign direct investment would increase, which would in turn mop up the unemployed. Quite Easily Done (QED). Think of Gear as the South African equivalent of a rising tide that lifts all.

This technocratic approach extended to each and every major policy decision and thus contributed to some of Mbeki's tragic mistakes, particularly his technical splitting of hairs around HIV/ AIDS, despite the historical and empirical evidence staring him in the face. The problem with technocracy is that it requires a certain

9 James C. Scott, *Seeing like a State*, 5

degree of authoritarianism to get everyone to walk in step. Mbeki bestrode the South African body politic like a political and technical colossus, leaving adult men and women, many of whom had feared nothing during the struggle, shaking in their shoes. This he did not achieve by any application of brute power but through the pretence of 'intellectual formidability'. He left many otherwise reasonably intelligent people dazzled: 'Oh, that guy can think, man' or 'He is so profound.' His state of the nation address was a display of statistical mastery, and his put-down of journalists – who tiptoed round him during interviews – fearsome. Although Jacob Zuma was part of the ANC leadership at the time, he did not do much to call Mbeki to order either – until Mbeki turned on him.

Will Zuma respect history?

Jacob Zuma has come on to the political stage less as a historic and more as a historical figure. Unlike Mbeki, who outmanoeuvred every contender for the title of heir to Nkrumah, Nasser, Nyerere and Mandela, Zuma is a historical actor in the way most of us are. By our little actions and pronouncements we shape and reshape the history of our world on a daily basis. Sometimes these actions coalesce into social movements for rebellion. The individuals who participate in a march are not historic actors in the same way as a Nelson Mandela or Barack Obama. However, they are historical actors who make change possible. Jacob Zuma seems to have had a sense of history in ways that Mbeki never did. After fifteen years of marginalisation and alienation, the 'wretched of the earth' saw in Zuma their anti-establishment symbol, forgetting that he had served in the establishment for all those years. Take a look around the world and you will see other populist figures like Zuma. Anwar Ibrahim was the deputy prime minister of Malaysia before his former mentor threw him in jail; Mir-Hossein Mousavi served as prime minister of Iran in the 1980s before he fell out with the clerical establishment.

Like many of the people who mobilised around him, Zuma came from a rural background, never went to school, fought in the liberation wars, worshipped in an African traditional church, had more than one wife, and seemed just like the ordinary guy next door. He brings to mind the example of the American war hero George Marshall, who gave his name to the post-war Marshall Plan for Europe. According to Neustadt and May, Marshall had a deep sense of history or what they call an appreciation of 'time as a stream' with a past, present and future. For example, during the Chinese civil war the Americans naturally supported the Nationalists against the Communists. Seeing that the Communists were gaining the upper hand, many people advised that the United States should send in troops. Marshall resisted the idea, arguing that such a move would lead to 'obligations and responsibilities ... which I am convinced the American people would never knowingly accept'. He argued that sending in the troops would be 'a continuing operation for a long time to come. It would involve this government in a continuing commitment from which it would practically be impossible to withdraw.'[10] Marshall thus allowed whatever sense he had of himself as a historic actor to be disciplined by historical realities and the historical sensibilities of his people. This sense of history was absent in American policy towards Vietnam and, more recently, in George Bush's invasion of Iraq. It was absent in Mbeki's denial of the experience of his people.

Marshall's sense of history or of thinking in time streams did not necessarily make him conservative and afraid of taking bold action. In fact it was his sense of history – more than any academic qualification – that led him to draw up the Marshall Plan: 'perhaps the boldest act of his whole career was the espousal of what history remembers as the Marshall Plan. After less than six months in the Secretaryship of State, though little acquainted before with either international economic issues or the people allegedly expert about them, Marshall

10 Ernest May and Richard Neustadt, *Thinking in Time*, 249.

concluded that economic conditions in Europe called for drastic and unprecedented remedies. Others, of course, provided diagnoses and suggested possible treatments. But the particular prescription was his own.[11]

At the press conference announcing his cabinet, a journalist asked Jacob Zuma what had informed his decisions: was it his experience as head of ANC intelligence? Zuma gave his characteristic chuckle and asked the journalist why he focused on only that aspect of his life. The president said his decision could just as well have been influenced by the experience of growing up herding cattle (which I imagine involved a great deal of patience). While Zuma successfully ducked the question, the journalist had in a way highlighted the fact that our social and cultural experiences and identities do not disappear simply because a new political order has come into being. Similarly, the temperament of our leaders was formed by the time we got to 1994. The interesting question is always how these social and cultural experiences interact with the political system to produce a political culture. The policy question is whether Jacob Zuma will be able to transfer that sense of history into the domain of public leadership.

Zuma has had remarkably good press since he assumed office. I would even say that the last time there was any such good press for a president was when Nelson Mandela was in office. The most celebrated aspect of Zuma's leadership is his willingness to listen. That's a great and commendable feat if he is going to avoid the temptations of would-be historic figures who want to change the world as they wish, but a historical figure alive to the experience of his people. Early indications are that Zuma is less intellectually pretentious or presumptuous than his predecessor. He likes to joke about the fact that he never went to school. But already there have been calls for him to be a leader who steps out in front to solve the nation's problems, especially in the wake of the community protests

11 Ibid., 249.

that rocked the country just as he was assuming power. The minister of human settlements, Tokyo Sexwale, rightly pointed out that the protests could not possibly be a reflection of the failure of Zuma's government, which had been elected only a few months previously. But people do not make such rational distinctions when they are taking to the streets. In their minds they are protesting against the government.

In what can be interpreted as an implied criticism of the Mbeki era, Zuma opined that the protests indicated that something had indeed gone horribly wrong in the relations between the government and the people. Instead of addressing the people on television or through government-orchestrated imbizos as Mbeki had done, he paid surprise visits to the communities caught up in the protests, just as he personally visited the places affected by xenophobic violence. Zuma has even invited some of his fiercest political critics into his office as part of his regular interactions with the country's intellectuals, black and white, men and women. Now the even greater challenge for Zuma is to institutionalise this leadership trait in order to change the way the government relates to its citizens.

Institutionalising democracy: the cabinet
Zuma's choice of cabinet ministers was reassuring. He brought together a diverse selection of individuals not only from different backgrounds but also from different constituencies within the ANC. The political analyst Steven Friedman distinguished Zuma from Mbeki in this way: 'Part of Mbeki's undoing was his refusal to accommodate all views within the ANC in his government. He also refused to reshuffle his Cabinet, alienating ambitious politicians. Zuma knows how politically damaging this can be and is anxious to signal to everyone in the ANC that they are included.'[12] Zuma's

12 Steven Friedman, 'Early days but Zuma shows signs of presidential promise', *Business Day*, 18 August 2009.

cabinet appointments were described by Anthony Butler as follows: 'his ministerial appointments, particularly in the economic realm, have exhibited real political dexterity'. Butler continued: 'Zuma has also changed the tone of national politics. Frustrated citizens who spent more than a decade having their concerns about corruption, HIV/AIDS, crime and the education system dismissed out of hand have been disarmed by his openness and ready ear.'[13] In an interview on e-tv, Mamphela Ramphele argued that 'President Jacob Zuma has got great people skills, and has the anxiety to leave a legacy. And this is one area where he is very competent and can succeed.'[14]

Even more important is Zuma's preparedness to let members of his cabinet take more responsibility for their portfolios, and not have to look over their shoulders. While some of the individual fits do not seem at all explicable, let alone inspiring – how does one explain the duo of Lulu Xingwana and Paul Mashatile at Arts and Culture, for instance? – a helicopter view of the cabinet gives one the confidence that it is unlikely that a stupid policy can emerge from such a group of people without its being hotly contested and disputed. Zuma seems to have the self-confidence to include strong, contrarian figures, including political rivals, around the table. Not only does this provide him with a form of political insurance but it also avoids the lone warrior model of leadership that characterised the Mbeki years. As Ronald Heifetz argues, 'the myth of leadership is the myth of the lone warrior: the solitary individual whose heroism and brilliance enable him to lead the way.' This ability to stand alone is important if the leader is to avoid the dependency or work-avoidance that afflicts people when they are under stress. But dependency cannot be completely erased because it is only human that from time to time 'people need to rest the weight of their burden on someone's shoulders'.[15]

13 Anthony Butler, 'Zuma has a way before he can be called a new deal', *Business Day*, 17 August 2009.
14 Mamphela Ramphele interview on e.tv with Dennis Davis, 18 June 2009.
15 Ronald Heifetz, *Leadership without Easy Answers* (Cambridge, MA: Harvard University Press, 1998), 251

Since taking office, Zuma has come under criticism from opposition leaders for not asserting himself. They demand that he should step out in front and put out political fires, such as the public sector strikes that gripped the country in mid-2009. My own feeling is that this response is indicative of South Africans reverting to type, looking to the leader to solve our problems, and I advised Zuma to reject such calls.[16]

This is a plea to President Jacob Zuma to please ignore the hypochondriacs. These are the people who are so dependent on the idea of the leader as the 'big man' that they are now having withdrawal symptoms. This reliance on the big man or 'die hoofleier' or 'the chief' lies deep in the history of this country. It's a political culture we inherited from Jan van Riebeeck right through to all those vainglorious 19th-century colonial governors. The history of the twentieth century is littered with these big men, and they were all men – Louis Botha, Jan Christiaan Smuts, D.F. Malan, Hendrik Verwoerd, John Vorster, P.W. Botha and F.W. de Klerk.

I may have missed some of these unlikeable characters but I'm sure you get the drift. Dan O'Meara illustrates this culture brilliantly in his book *Forty Lost Years,* the best thing written on the history of the National Party. O'Meara also makes the observation, first made by Steve Biko in the 1970s, that people like Verwoerd went beyond just Afrikaner nationalism in the construction of an overarching culture of white supremacy that included English-speaking whites.

In his brilliant column on this page yesterday Steven Friedman describes how the pervasiveness of white supremacist thinking produced a culture that always treats black people as suspect and gives the benefit of the doubt to the worst white people. Indeed how does an unreconstructed racist such as David Bullard achieve the

16 Xolela Mangcu, 'Zuma must beware the booby-trapped calls for leadership', *Business Day*, 16 July 2009.

status of a superstar in the white community? Well, in the same way that a white person with a Standard Four could spit in the face of a black doctor or lawyer and be decorated as a hero.

Just as this society and its institutions have taken white mediocrity to be the standard, we have inherited the reliance on 'die hoofleier' or 'the chief' in the democratic era. Our evolution over the past ten years was shepherded by two very different big men – Nelson Mandela and Thabo Mbeki. I shall resist the temptation to elaborate on the differences. Let's just say one was tall and one was short – literally and figuratively.

The absurdity of the 'big man' logic is that Jacob Zuma is expected to solve every major problem we otherwise cannot solve. And if he should fail, then he would have failed as a leader, which would then confirm what the Bullards secretly wished for in the first place – so that all manner of racist stereotypes could then be confirmed.

While the pleas for 'leadership' may sound the most reasonable thing for citizens to ask of a president, they are actually not that innocent. In reality these are pleas not just for Zuma to intervene but to intervene on the side of those who make the pleas. Clever. But don't take the bait, Mr President. Instead, provide the platform for us to work out our problems. If all the legacy you left was a nation in conversation with itself in search of solutions for its problems, then you would have done more than most presidents in history.

There will no doubt be times when you have to make decisive interventions. But even as you do that, avoid the trap of seeming to have answers for everything. That would make you a pretender. People don't like pretenders. If you don't believe me, then ask your predecessor.

If I were to advise you on one thing it would be to recommend one of the best pieces I have ever read on political leadership. It's a chapter titled 'Neither Leaders Nor Followers' in *A Passion for Democracy* by Benjamin Barber.

Barber warns us about the idea of the leader as the big man thus: 'public officials displaying an omnicompetent mastery of their public responsibilities unburden private men and women of their responsibilities.' He warns that 'the people are apt to cry "what will we do without him" and doubt whether they can go on. What is really only a departure is experienced as a loss and an incapacitation.'

Frankly this is the stuff that makes presidents think they are indispensable, and gets them conspiring to extend their stay in office, by any means necessary. Who can blame them when we build them into the dictators we later decry? But if we cannot learn from our most recent history, then what shall be our guide?

The other criticism that commentators have made about Zuma is that it is only a matter of time before he behaves like most politicians. Richard Calland, for one, celebrates the glasnost emanating from the Zuma presidency: 'the paranoia and insecurity that were the hallmarks of the Mbeki era are, temporarily at least, vanquished. There is a self-confidence as well as a conviviality about the tone the new president is setting.'[17] Nonetheless, Calland urges us to prepare ourselves for the inevitability of disappointment: 'This is not to cast aspersions on the good intentions of the Zuma Cabinet, or to adopt an unduly cynical attitude to contemporary politics, but rather to recognise that the challenges are so intense that it is all but impossible to do anything other than fail.'

Calland does not think he is being cynical at all, just realistic. In fact he thinks his realism may even be for our own good because it will help us lower our expectations and accept failure instead of crucifying politicians for their inevitable inability to meet our ever-escalating needs. Though I agree with Calland's caution about politicians, I disagree with his reasoning. In other words, there is nothing that automatically protects Zuma from what has afflicted political leaders

17 Richard Calland, 'A breath of fresh air', *Mail & Guardian*, 27 July 2009.

throughout history: the temptations and arrogance of power. For a political leader to resist such temptation requires not only sensibility to history but a whole variety of other political innovations as well, from his cabinet colleagues, parliamentarians, civil society and the media. Where I differ with Calland is with respect to his reasoning: I do not think that politicians are destined to fail. There are leaders who have used power for the social good, from Franklin D. Roosevelt to Nelson Mandela. Greatness is always a possibility in leaders, and our task as citizens is to urge them to reach for such greatness in the name of the greater good, and this starts by listening to criticism.

Listening, however, can cut both ways. While leaders can use listening as a way of deepening the democratic culture, they can also use it as an instrument for evasion. When Julius Malema raised the controversial matter of the composition of the economic cluster of the cabinet as being weighted by non-Africans, Zuma and the ANC secretary-general, Gwede Mantashe, responded by reading him the rule-book about the ANC as a non-racial organisation instead of engaging with the debate he was raising. In a sense they were right – and they were also defending the integrity of comrades who had given up so much for the party. Moreover, their response was a welcome departure from the racial nativism of the Mbeki years. But asserting a position and a solution does not make the problem go away. That is the same with Zuma's meeting with taxi owners who were unhappy that the government was introducing a Bus Rapid Transit system that would undermine their business. Zuma promised that the bus system would be suspended. However, months later the government announced that it was going ahead with the BRT system anyway. Could the taxi owners be faulted for thinking they had been 'played' while all along the president and the government proceeded with the implementation of the system?

The third criticism that is commonly made is that Zuma is all style and no substance. Patricia de Lille says we have a president who can do the song and dance but beyond this there is nothing. Helen Zille welcomed Zuma's inclusive leadership style but believed that he lacks the substance that makes a great leader. As Anthony Butler observed: 'when it comes to matters of substance, however, it is too early to tell if Zuma can help the society's deeper ills.' What is more, the differences that separate Zuma and Mbeki, Butler avers, are just a matter of style rather than being substantively ideological.[18]

I would like to dwell on this last type of criticism, partly because I spent a few years of my life arguing against its assumptions in my doctoral dissertation. The dissertation was about a piece of urban history that is not well known in South Africa but has been widely followed in the US, Latin America and certain European cities. It is the story of the election of Harold Washington as the first black mayor of Chicago. Just as we must look back in time, we must also look across spaces for the resolution of our problems. Human experience is not so divergent over time and space.

The power of symbolic action: from Harold Washington to Barack Obama

When I first arrived at Cornell I was intrigued by a book that my adviser Pierre Clavel and Wim Wiewel had edited on the experience of Harold Washington, the first black mayor of the city of Chicago. The book described Washington's period of governance as 'one of the high points in the history of American cities ... his reforms marked the end of the notorious machine identified with Richard J. Daley.'[19] I was intrigued by the argument that Harold Washington's critics made, that his administration was all style and no substance and that he had left economic relations unchanged in the city. This, by the way, is the same scepticism that has been expressed about Barack Obama: that his policies will not fundamentally alter power relations

18 Anthony Butler, *Business Day*, 17 August 2009.
19 Pierre Clavel and Wim Wiewel, *Harold Washington and the Neighbourhoods: Progressive City Government in Chicago, 1983–1987* (New Brunswick: Rutgers, 1991), 1.

both within the United States and between the United States and the rest of the world.

While I shall return to this theme in the following chapter, suffice it to say for now that it reveals a constricted view of what matters to people. Human society and human experience cannot be reduced to the economy, crucial as that is to our livelihoods. Surely an experience such as the election of the first African American president in the history of the United States must count for something? Surely, too, the Harold Washington administration must have counted for something for those people who had been excluded for decades from city government? It is that 'something' that was absent in the evaluations of Washington's administration. Most of the analyses, both positive and negative, came from white scholars who, like their progressive counterparts in South Africa, analysed the black world in purely material terms. They had no sense of history, or at least of black history. To be sure, while there are many white people who understood the historical importance of Washington's achievement for black people, on the whole the cultural dimension got the short end of the stick in evaluations. What Thomas Sergiovanni has said about the lack of attention to the relationship between leadership and symbolic action was particularly true of studies of Harold Washington: 'studies of leadership give too much attention to the instrumental and behavioral aspects and not enough to the symbolic and cultural'.[20]

I suppose my attention or sensitivity to the non-economic dimensions of human existence is a reflection of my being reared in the black consciousness movement in South Africa. In *Pedagogy of Hope*, a sequel to *Pedagogy of the Oppressed*, Paolo Freire criticised the economistic, technocratic approach to life: 'We are surrounded by a pragmatic discourse that would have us adapt to the facts of

20 Thomas Sergiovanni and John E. Corbally, *Leadership and Organizational Culture: New Perspectives on Administrative Theory and Practice* (Urbana: University of Illinois Press, 1998), 12.

reality. Dreams and Utopia are not only called useless but positively impeding.' Freire warned that 'the attempt to do without hope, in the struggle to improve the world, as if that struggle could be reduced to calculated acts alone, or a purely scientific approach, is a frivolous illusion'.[21] Instead of seeing the economy as the determining force in social life, scholars such as Karl Polanyi turned the logic on its head. In fact, for Polanyi most social disasters and calamities are preceded by the destruction of the cultural and institutional base of the victims: 'Not economic exploitation, as often assumed, but the disintegration of the cultural environment of the victim is then the cause of the degradation.'[22] In *The Great Arch*, Phillip Corrigan and Derek Sayer describe the capitalist revolution as not just an economic phenomenon but as a wholesale revolution in the way the world is made sense of.[23]

Similarly, the struggle of black people in Chicago was not just a series of calculated acts or a scientific, economic endeavour. The hope for a better life – to borrow a much-used South African phrase – was not separate from the desire for political self-determination: political participation was not seen as marginal but as constitutive of the very essence of a meaningful life. And this was the promise of the Harold Washington moment in Chicago's long and notoriously racist history, a racism that rested on the twin pillars of corruption and autocratic rule under the leadership of Richard Daley, who ran the city like a personal fiefdom from 1955 to 1975. Black people fleeing the racism of the American South looked to Chicago for hopes of a different world. They came to Chicago because it was then the 'hog butcher of the world' and the centre of world trade. However, their hopes soon turned out to be a cruel illusion as they soon found themselves on the

21 Paulo Freire, *Pedagogy of Hope: Reliving Pedagogy of the Oppressed* (New York: Continuum, 1996), 8.
22 Karl Polanyi, *The Great Transformation* (Boston: Beacon Press, 1957).
23 Philip Corrigan and Derek Sayer, *The Great Arch: English State Formation as Cultural Revolution* (New York: Blackwell Publishers, 1985), 1–2.

receiving end of an equally virulent and violent racism in their newly found home. Not surprisingly, Chicago also became, in the words of Richard Wright, 'the city from which the most incisive and radical Negro thought has come'.[24]

Harold Washington – and later Barack Obama – came out of that history. Both Washington and Obama were not radical activists in any way but they benefited from the radical-militant tradition of Chicago. Washington rose through the ranks of the notorious political machine that ran the city. He was always independent, biding his time before challenging the machine. After a series of stops and starts, including humiliating losses at the polls, Washington was finally drafted to run for mayor in 1983 by black militant activists under the leadership of Lu Palmer. In a packed Bethel AME church he was chosen as the community's favourite candidate.

By this time Washington had obtained a seat in Congress and was reluctant to give it up. His condition for acceptance was that the campaign organisers should register a minimum of 50,000 voters before he would even consider running for mayor. The veteran *Chicago Tribune* columnist Vernon Jarrett described the subsequent voter registration drive as 'the supreme moment of black unity in the history of this city'. Groups and individuals went out almost spontaneously, unbeknown to each other, running around registering voters. Washington's election as the first black mayor of this notoriously racist city was described by the Chicago writer Studs Terkel as an American 'Soweto'.

In his autobiography, *Dreams from My Father*, Barack Obama describes how his barber, Smitty, reacted to Washington's victory:

the night Harold won, let me tell you, people ran the streets. It was like the day Joe Louis knocked out Schmeling. Same feeling. People

24 St Clair Drake and Horace Cayton, *Black Metropolis: A Study of Negro Life in a Northern City* (Chicago: University of Chicago Press, 1945).

weren't just proud of Harold. They were proud of themselves. I stayed inside, but my wife and I, we couldn't go to bed until three, we were so excited. When I woke up in the morning, it seemed like the most beautiful day of my life. [25]

In my dissertation I described some of the changes in city government that the Washington administration brought about. For the most part these were institutional changes in the way local government was run: from the incestuous, corrupt practices that had been the basis of local government for the previous five decades to an opening up of local government to communities. His very first step was to appoint a black police chief, something unheard of in the history of the city.

Washington was not fazed by the hostility from the all-white city council. He went above them, directly, to the most hostile white communities. They would boo and jeer but he kept coming to their conventions and community meetings and would sometimes stay right into the night. He undercut his racist opponents by reaching out to the most racist neighbourhoods in the city, just to listen and engage with them. The result was that one of his most vocal opponents, Jean Mayer of the suggestively titled 'Save Our Neighbourhoods' Coalition, became one of the mayor's leading supporters in the city.

Washington expected his senior officials to be with him at his meetings, patiently explaining the details of his policy proposals, including an innovative approach to the city budgeting process that opened it up to all city residents. This was unheard of in a city where the machine bosses had carved up city projects among themselves for decades. Washington also used one of his major institutional innovations, 'the mayoral task force', to co-opt some of his opponents into the city's decision-making structures. By the end of his first term about two thousand people had participated in these

25 Barack Obama, *Dreams from My Father* (New York: Random House, 2004), 148.

task forces. Community groups became part of the city's planning and budget processes. According to Doug Gills, 'it was now possible to find out what was happening in the city to a far greater extent than ever happened before. It made sense from a community activist standpoint to be able to walk into Harold's office. It made sense to be able to pick up the phone and talk to the commissioner of economic development.'[26]

Washington demonstrated through word and symbolic action that people could be mobilised to participate in the structures that made decisions about their lives. In the end he proved that a black-led but diverse city could prove more efficient than the closed, corrupt culture that the racists were trying to preserve. Indeed, the city's bond rating improved under his watch, and city government became more professional than it had ever been.

The point of this diversion into the history of Chicago is that what is often dismissed as just a matter of style has substantive consequences in public policy. As the distinguished foreign policy analyst Fareed Zakaria puts it in his book, *The Post-American World*, 'policy matters but so does the symbolism around it.' Zakaria illustrates the difference between George Bush's and Barack Obama's style and the substantive impact of each. Beginning with Bush, he notes:

President Bush's foreign trips seem designed to require as little contact as possible with the countries he visits. He is usually accompanied by two thousand or so Americans, as well as several airplanes, helicopters and cars. He sees little except palaces and conference rooms. His trips involve almost no effort to demonstrate respect and appreciation for the country and culture he is visiting. They also rarely involve any meetings with people outside the government – the businessmen, civil society leaders, activists. Even though the president's visit must

26 In Xolela Mangcu, 'Harold Washington and the cultural transformation of local government in Chicago' PhD, Cornell University, 1997.

be highly programmed by definition, a broader effort to touch the people in those foreign lands would have great symbolic value.[27]

The style became part of the substance when Barack Obama took over. Obama has demonstrated a calm humility that bespeaks an inner peace and strength. One could see this style of leadership at work when he stood up to greet Venezuela's leader Hugo Chávez or when he responded to an attack on the United States by saying he was not there when all the terrible things being said about his country took place. A few days after the meeting with the Venezuelan leader, Chávez agreed to send an envoy to the United States, for the first time in many years. Obama has also sent out signals of his intention to end the American embargo against Cuba. One of his first actions in office was his decision to close the prison at Guantánamo Bay. Addressing the Turkish parliament he boldly announced that America was not an enemy of Islam. He took the same message to Cairo. On his visit to Ghana he implored Africans to create democratic institutions instead of relying on big men as leaders.

No one in the world is a greater example of the power of symbolic leadership than Nelson Mandela. Mandela sought to reassure whites through various other symbolic acts, all of which relied on the theme of non-racialism. His intervention to calm the nation after the assassination of the much-loved Chris Hani was just one example by which he tried to demonstrate to the nation that even though the killer was a white person, the person who identified him was a white woman: 'a white man full of prejudice and hate, came to our country and committed a deed so foul that our whole nation teeters on the brink of disaster. A white woman, of Afrikaner origin, risked her life so that we may know, and bring to justice, this assassin.'[28]

Mandela visited the ailing wife of the apartheid architect, Hendrik

27 Faried Zakaria, *The Post-American World* (New York: W.W. Norton, 2008), 225.
28 Anthony Sampson, *Mandela: The Authorised Biography* (London: HarperCollins, 2000), 469.

Verwoerd, as well as Percy Yutar, the prosecutor responsible for his lengthy imprisonment. He added to his presidential security team the prison warder who had watched over him during his years of incarceration. He came out in full support of the almost all-white rugby team that won the rugby World Cup in 1995, donning the team's colours when he came out on the field to greet the players. Through all of these actions Mandela seemed acutely aware that on his shoulders rested the prospects of an entire country, not just its economy but its entire social existence with all the continuities and changes that go with such an epochal transition.

I was one of those who criticised Mandela for bending over backwards to white people without getting anything in return. But perhaps he had 'a sense of time as a stream'; that whatever he did in the present would lay the foundations for future action. Inevitably, he must have felt, black people would come to assert themselves over other aspects of our national life and white people would come to appreciate the necessity of change. Mandela's contribution has been to make the initial political opening possible in real and materially significant ways.

Jacob Zuma is a very different politician from Harold Washington, Barack Obama and Nelson Mandela, all of whom are polished lawyers. He does, however, seem to share one trait with them: a commitment to Nelson Mandela's legacy. He has come on to the stage by reaffirming history. In every major speech he has begun by making a link with the legacy of inclusivity and patience with one's detractors that characterised Mandela's leadership. Like Mandela he has started out by making special visits to poor working-class Afrikaner families, and he appointed to his cabinet Pieter Mulder, the leader of the pro-Afrikaner Freedom Front party. He has avoided the race bait, even when offered by some of his colleagues, as in the discussion about minorities provoked by the ANC Youth League. While any populist leader would have jumped at the opportunity to strengthen his support base by appealing to its baser instincts, Zuma did not.

Building a sense of community agency and ownership

The argument for style and symbolism is not an argument against substance and transformation. There are many substantive thematic lessons that Zuma can take from our rich and varied history. The black consciousness movement's emphasis on community agency and self-reliance could be a useful antidote to the crippling concept of service delivery that has been the short-hand for development over the past fifteen years. There has never been a more propitious time for the theme of self-reliance that informed the black consciousness movement. One of that movement's enduring arguments is that black people need to have a sense of ownership over their destinies – and I would imagine over their own country. In the early 1970s Barney Pityana expressed the animating philosophy behind the movement as follows: 'It is essential for the black students to strive to elevate the level of consciousness of the black community by promoting awareness, pride and capabilities.'[29] For the next decade Pityana and his colleagues initiated community projects – under the umbrella of the Black Community Programmes – that spanned the arts, education, culture, the economy, politics and the media. They played a crucial role in the famous Durban dockworker strike of 1973. The Zanempilo Health Clinic run by Mamphela Ramphele became a celebrated model for community-based health care.

Some time ago I interviewed a priest from the Eastern Cape, Mcebisi Xundu, about the black consciousness movement. He explained to me that the reason for the projects was not only material improvement of people's lives. Once people had a sense of ownership of something, they would fight to defend it. A black consciousness publication,

29 Barney Pityana cited in Xolela Mangcu, 'Social movements and city planning', Cornell Working Papers, Department of City and Regional Planning, Cornell University, 1993.

Black Review, suggested that in evaluating community projects it was necessary to look beyond the structures. Even more important was the level of consciousness attained by the groups involved. The purpose of such projects had been not only to provide gainful employment to destitute people but also to train people in mastering certain basic production and management skills and in mastering their own lives. They also provided the basis for communal action.

As I have argued, something was lost in the transition from organisation building in the 1970s to mass mobilisation in the 1980s. I make a distinction between organisation and mobilisation. Organisation is sustained building of relationships and constituencies over a period of time. Mobilisation can easily turn into rabble-rousing that achieves what it sets out to do but leaves nothing behind. These days I often feel we are still experiencing the loss of organisation, which was the hallmark of the black consciousness movement in the 1970s. I said as much in a column in reaction to the trashing of streets by striking workers in mid-2009.[30]

The season of strikes is closely coming to an end, and we need to reflect on what it is we need to do to break this annual cycle of strikes. In doing so we should be wary of valorising protest when it is in fact an indication that something is wrong. We should also make a distinction between protest under apartheid and protest as a constitutional right in a democratic society. The violent nature of the protests raises questions that have often been raised with respect to the violent nature of crime in this country. We are certainly not the only country where citizens protest against their government, and where the protests turn violent. This happens all the time in Europe. But I can't quite imagine the French trashing the Louvre. I am not a psychologist or anything of the sort but a person can only destroy property if they have no sense of

30 Xolela Mangcu, 'Reaping the whirlwind of another decade of estrangement', *Business Day*, 6 August 2009.

ownership or investment in it. In a sense there is a break in the opening line of the Freedom Charter: 'South Africa belongs to all who live in it …' Only the second half of that sentence has any closeness to reality. We simply live here but do not see this place as belonging to us.

I have often argued that we are reaping the whirlwind of a technocratic approach to development. The situation may even be worse. We are reaping the whirlwind of a lack of attention to what turns countries into nations – from a mere scattering of individuals to a shared sense of national identity. Over the past ten years we have had a bifurcated identity between those who appropriated the country to themselves under the leadership of Thabo Mbeki, and those who lived on the margins of that society – not only economically but also psychologically. It would be folly to think that the election of Jacob Zuma four months ago would have removed that sense of estrangement …

What could we possibly do as a society to respond to the alienation? First, we have to go back to the basics of building political community and create what Gandhi called 'building bridges with the people'. But what it also means was that when Jacob Zuma goes to a 'hotspot' there must be someone on the other side to meet with. These are the civic and trade union leaders who have seemed rather helpless as their supporters rampaged through the streets as if there was no tomorrow. This is therefore not just a party/government issue but a civic challenge that requires consciousness raising on the scale last seen during the black consciousness movement of the 1970s. The movement used to have formation schools – where community leaders regularly met to provide political education and leadership training to community leaders who would then take that out into the streets.

The irony about the trade union movement in this country is that it has become so economistic. This is not to say that the wage demands are not fair – they most probably are legitimate. But is there really no way we can also have a broader conversation about citizenship and nation building led by trade union leaders themselves? After all, these are the very same people who argued against economism in the 1980s – arguing that shop floor issues were not separate from community and national issues.

Jacob Zuma has taken the lead by engaging with the people seeing the protests as an indication that something has broken down. There can be no clearer break from the disdain for communities that characterised the Mbeki regime. Where Mbeki's instinct was to question, deny and even ridicule critics, Zuma's instinct has been to listen. However, building active citizenship is a global challenge that should be at the heart of our foreign policy. That's an idea worth the consideration of our newly appointed ambassadors.

Is the National Planning Commission enough

Thus far the assumption in this chapter has been that we can make government leaders sensitive to history and that we can make government responsive without changing the way it is structured. But can we really? In his classic work *Leadership and Administration*, Philip Selznick makes a distinction between organisations and institutions.[31] He sees institutionalisation as the process by which the leadership of an organisation helps build the commitment of group members to the goals, objectives, methods and world view of the organisation. Selznick proposed four criteria by which this institutionalisation proceeds. Firstly, the leadership needs to establish a new definition and role for the organisation. Secondly, it has to achieve what he calls the institutional embodiment of purpose. Thirdly, a new organisational design should be elaborated to focus on the most critical tasks for realising organisational values. Specialised units need to be created to protect the precarious values of the organisation. These units would be high up in the organisational leadership to protect them

31 Philip Selznick, *Leadership in Administration: A Sociological Interpretation* (Evanston, IL: Row, Peterson, 1957).

from attack by other units in the organisation. Fourthly, mechanisms should be devised for the mediation of internal conflict.

It is not difficult to see how such a schematic way of doing things could be adapted to institutional innovation in South Africa. The first criterion is par for the course: every leader must bring to government a sense of what's important to them. Secondly, the institutional embodiment of purpose can be achieved through the symbolic leadership I have described above. Harold Washington embodied a new type of Chicago, just as Jacob Zuma has come to embody a more open government. The third element of Selznick's schematic framework has been achieved through the institution of the National Planning Commission, a place where the precarious values of the organisation are being pursued and protected, right in the presidency and by one of the most powerful individuals of the past decade, Trevor Manuel.

Selznick came under heavy criticism for his centralising tendencies and for his preoccupation with the defensive needs of the organisation against insecurity, instability and heterogeneity. The sociologist Alvin Gouldner put it this way: 'these contrary needs are just as real and just as consequential for organizational behavior as those proposed by Selznick. But they point in a different direction. They are oriented to problems of change, of growth, of challenging contingencies, of provoking and unsettling encounters. Selznick's analysis seems to imply that survival is possible only in icy stasis, in which security, continuity and stability are the key terms.'[32]

The responsible minister, Trevor Manuel, has assured us that the National Planning Commission will not adopt a centralised approach to planning in the tradition of the failed Soviet model. But that's an easy one. The more difficult challenge is how to overcome the elite and technocratic impulse. As James C. Scott pointed out in *Seeing*

32 Alvin Gouldner, 'Metaphysical pathos and the theory of bureaucracy', *American Political Science Review*, 49 (1955), 496–507.

like a State, this is neither a left-wing nor a right-wing problem. High modernism lies at the epistemological foundations of both doctrines. To the extent that the newly created Planning Commission reproduces this particular approach to public decision-making, it will be no more than a reversion to the Mbeki years – as well as a throw-back to planning traditions that predate bold experiments such as the Chicago example under Harold Washington. The real question is whether the Planning Commission can sponsor the kind of community-based planning initiatives that have been carried out in countries as varied as the United States, India and Brazil.

Institutionalising deliberative practice

Speaking at the Platform for Public Deliberation, the deputy general secretary of the Communist Party and deputy minister of transport, Jeremy Cronin, was asked what made South Africa unique in the world. He replied that it is the ability to work together across fault-lines. I summed it up as our 'deliberative strength'.[33]

There is ample historical and empirical evidence that planners and policy-makers can be more effective in their work through listening and deliberating with communities. John Forester, a senior member of the faculty of city planning at Cornell, argues that planners can foster public deliberation in at least three ways. Firstly, there is the power that comes from technical expertise – bringing professional knowledge to bear in the deliberative process. This requires attentiveness to what others have to say, with a clear readiness to change one's path if the situation calls for it. Forester describes this as the process of downgrading 'the image of your own profession' as opposed to being Mr or Ms Know-All. This in turn requires a preparedness to know what you do not know and to learn through deliberation. While one can go to graduate school to acquire technical skills, deliberation

33 Jeremy Cronin, Address at the Platform for Public Deliberation, University of Johannesburg, 7 April 2008.

requires the humility to listen and respect people holding different views. This is not listening for listening's sake but listening with the demonstrated willingness to do something about the perspective of others. Forester argues that social groups invariably yearn for 'diplomatic recognition'. This is particularly the case when people are divided by their social identities. Failing to listen to someone can be taken as a denial of their very identity. He quotes one of the planners he interviewed for his book *Deliberative Planning*:

> I would say that the main thing, really, is that when you give other people 'diplomatic recognition', even as a tactic, it changes them. It's like international relations: the handshake between Rabin and Arafat has a significance far beyond the fact that Arafat and Rabin shook hands. It changes them. Neither of them is going to be the same for that handshake. I think it's the same in planning. When you give other people 'diplomatic recognition' professionally, even as a tactic to soften them up, you end up changing too. Because then you, having recognized them, have to take them seriously.[34]

Jacob Zuma was able to calm a potentially crippling strike of taxi owners by simply showing up to listen to them. But he did not only listen; he did something about their concerns by suspending the development of a bus system that the taxi owners said would deprive them of their livelihood. He gave them diplomatic recognition. (This did not quell the strikes, though.)

Forester argues that the second way to foster deliberative planning is by taking the time to think about the short-term and long-term consequences of today's actions: thinking in time streams. Thirdly, Forester attaches a great deal of value to the process of design in planning, not only the way meetings are conducted but how this

---

34 John Forester, *The Deliberative Practitioner: Encouraging Participatory Planning Processes* (Cambridge, MA: MIT Press, 1999), 108.

is done over a long period of time. The African novelist Ayi Kwei Armah calls for creative design in fostering development. He argues that new creative designers can be creative only when they have access to, and not just professional knowledge of, a broader memory bank of words, ideas, values, experiences and mythologies. We must have a sense of history because 'our history contains a record, a reservoir of suggestions for methods, strategies and approaches for solving the problems we are now living under. If we were in full possession of all this intelligence, we would be very good designers, we would be problem-solvers for our own society...'[35] This echoes an argument made in a different context by Alan Altshuler that the social problems we often encounter are not new: with a little bit of digging we may find how people solved them or who was able to solve them.[36]

As far as the National Planning Commission is concerned, Steven Friedman is right: the effectiveness of the Commission will not be measured by the extent to which it gets other government departments to stay within budgets in a top-down approach. Its effectiveness can only come from a realisation that the work of government takes place outside government and in cultivating the processes of deliberation among culturally and socially diverse groups of people – as Harold Washington did in Chicago or Barack Obama may still do in the United States.

In the next chapter I discuss the similarities between Obama's and Zuma's challenges. Both of them came into power on the back of popular rebellions, during a time when economic certitudes could no longer provide solutions to the world's problems, and the challenge of institutional innovation for popular participation in government was at its greatest. Although this is a challenge that both countries need to meet individually, by working together they could lead a new

35 Ayi Kwei Armah, Public lecture at the Human Sciences Research Council, 25 February 2005.
36 Alan Altshuler, *City Planning Process: A Political Analysis* (Ithaca: Cornell University Press, 1965).

agenda for active citizenship in the world. I argue that our foreign policy needs to be rethought to include this challenge. Besides, there is much that links the United States and South Africa. There are no two more similar countries in terms of our racial history, the history of our political movements, the urban culture, and the linkages that have existed over time. The next chapter is therefore an examination of how we in South Africa and southern Africa should relate to the United States and become part of a new movement for global change.

Building active citizenship at home and abroad: towards a transatlantic alliance on active citizenship

The ties that bind

If Harold Washington's election as the first black mayor of Chicago was an American 'Soweto', then Barack Obama's election as the first black president of the United States was a global 'Soweto'. No American election has ever elicited as much global interest, and no presidential candidate has ever received as much global goodwill as Barack Obama. The invocation of the black township of Soweto where hundreds of students were killed by racist police in 1976 is deliberate. I am always struck by the political similarities and the cultural affinities between black South Africans and African Americans. From slavery to the civil rights era, African Americans lived as second-class citizens in the country of their birth. In 1857 the US Supreme Court ruled in the *Dred Scott* v *Sandford* case that people of African descent and their descendants could not be American citizens. It took the American Civil War to bring the system of chattel slavery to an end. Momentary relief came with the onset of the period of Reconstruction (1866–77) when African American men were given the right to vote. A tiny minority were elected into state legislatures and Congress including the United States Senate. But the promise of freedom, justice and independence soon turned into the nightmare of Jim Crow in the South (1877–1965). Ira Katznelson describes Jim Crow as 'a combination of social conventions, racist ideas, economic compulsion, theological justification, political institutions, and harsh enforcement by police, the courts, and prisons, buttressed by private violence'.[1]

While we should always be careful not to transpose historical experiences between countries – precisely because no two experiences are ever the same – Katznelson's definition could easily have been that of apartheid South Africa. It amounted to what Steve Biko repeatedly described as the totality of the white power structure in South Africa.[2] This history of racial oppression provided the basis for what Bernard Magubane called 'the ties that bind'[3] between African Americans and black South Africans. These links go back to the nineteenth century when South Africans such as W.B. Rubusana, John Dube, Charlotte Maxeke, Sol Plaatje, Pixley ka Seme, R.V. Selope Thema studied under and also collaborated with the likes of Booker T. Washington and W.E.B. DuBois. The similarities extend to the practices and discourses of struggle, with the notable exception of the armed struggle. The very same debates that raged in the civil rights movement in the United States between the non-racial integrationism of Martin Luther King and the militant black nationalism of Malcolm X also divided black South Africans between the non-racial, integrationist ANC of Nelson Mandela, on the one hand, and the militant nationalism of the Pan Africanist Congress and the black consciousness movement of Robert Sobukwe and Steve Biko, on the other.

African American organisations such as Randall Robinson's TransAfrica played a crucial role in mobilising people for sanctions

1 Ira Katznelson, *When Affirmative Action Was White: An Untold Story of Racial Inequality in 20th Century America* (New York: W.W. Norton, 2005), 5.
2 Steve Biko, *I Write What I Like* (Johannesburg, Picador, 2004).
3 Bernard Magubane, *The Ties That Bind: African American Consciousness of Africa* (Trenton, NJ: Africa World Press, 1987).

and divestment of American companies from apartheid South Africa. In *Dreams from My Father*, Barack Obama recalls as one of his formative political experiences a speech he gave at a divestment rally in college:

> There's a struggle going on. I say there's a struggle going on. It's happening an ocean away. But it's a struggle that touches each and every one of us. Whether we know it or not. Whether we want it or not. A struggle that demands we choose sides. Not between black and white. Not between rich and poor. No – it's a harder choice than that. It's a choice between dignity and servitude. Between fairness and injustice. Between commitment and indifference. A choice between right and wrong.

And then he became self-deprecating and self-critical: 'I don't believe that what happens to a kid in Soweto makes much difference to the people we were talking to. Pretty words don't make it so. So why do I pretend otherwise? I'll tell you why. Because it makes me feel important. Because I like the applause. It gives me a nice, cheap thrill. That's what I believe.'

One of his college friends saw the sincerity in him: 'Well, you could have fooled me. Seemed to me like I heard a man speak who believed in something. A black man who cared. But hey I guess I'm stupid.'[4] This was the discovery of his own political efficacy, and to this day Obama conveys this sense of sincerity.

It is equally true and unfortunate that an unspoken distance developed between the former liberation fighters in South Africa and their African American counterparts after 1994.[5] Whereas the

4 Barack Obama, *Dreams from My Father* (New York: Random House, 2004), 107–8.
5 There has been a similar distance from some of the countries that hosted our liberation fighters for decades. It is remarkable that it is only with the election of Jacob Zuma that South Africa has normalised relations with Angola, a country that more than any other hosted the ANC's liberation army.

ANC leadership had relied on African American support during the years of struggle and exile, in their new roles they almost completely shunned their former supporters. When Nelson Mandela first visited the United States after release from prison, he was introduced by the veteran community leader Mel King in Boston. Later I got to know Mel King as my professor at the Massachusetts Institute of Technology. King used to comment that the ANC leaders he had hosted throughout the struggle never bothered to come round to the community when they visited Boston. Their visits ended at Harvard or in Washington to discuss 'important matters of state'. This growing rift has only added to the ignorance in South Africa about the progressive dimension of American history.

What is more, no one in the ANC government was available to meet Barack Obama when he visited South Africa in 2006. Probably sensing the folly of it all, Trevor Manuel, who was then minister of finance, is reported to have met secretly with him. The only other person who met the future president was Archbishop Desmond Tutu, who was later awarded the Medal of Honor, the highest civilian medal bestowed by the US Congress. Nelson Mandela is the only other South African to have received the honour. Apparently Mbeki would not meet Obama because he was peeved with Obama for having criticised his government's controversial position on HIV/ AIDS. Mbeki apparently made this clear at a breakfast meeting for the Friends of the President golf tournament held at the Pretoria Country Club in 2007. According to the former Vodacom chairman, Oyama Mabandla, one of the sponsors of the tournament, Mbeki pulled no punches in his attack on Obama. 'I don't like that boy. He cannot come to our country and criticise us like that.' Mabandla's response was simple and straightforward: 'I beg to differ, Mr President, Barack Obama is the next big thing in American politics: sheer talent, Mr President, a phenomenon, and he is only 45.' By saying he was only 45, Mabandla meant to convey to Mbeki, who would have been twenty years Obama's senior, that he could still have met him and advised him about the imprudence of criticising his hosts. But that was not Mbeki's style. The only way he knew to deal with critics was to ostracise them. But Mabandla concludes with a tinge of sadness in his voice: 'But look at where Obama is now and where Mbeki is. Mbeki is out there in the wilderness and Obama is the most powerful man in the world.'[6] Obama asked to visit a township and to talk to students before returning to the United States. The idea that the ruling party would not make time for a Senator is remarkable in its own right, but even more unforgivable is that the man was the rising star of the Democratic Party, having delivered a riveting address as the keynote speaker at the Democratic National Convention in 2004.

Our ignorance of American progressive history would not have been assisted by the ascendancy of George W. Bush, who brought back images of America's past as a bully nation that acted independently of the rest of the international community. Under Bush's leadership the United States refused to sign international treaties such as the Kyoto Accord, recognise international institutions such as the International Criminal Court or even pay its dues to the United Nations. Against the caution of the United Nations and other world leaders, America found its way into the quagmire of the Iraq war. In short, under Bush America lost its standing as a global moral icon among the peoples of the world. I reflected on the implications of George Bush's decision to invade Iraq.[7]

The day after the September 11 bombings at the World Trade Center, America's most influential newspaper, the *New York Times*, observed that 'this is an age when even revenge is complicated, when it is hard to match the desire for retribution with the need for certainty. We suffer

6 Author interview with former Vodacom chairman Oyama Mabandla.
7 Xolela Mangcu, 'Reckless tyrant sacrifices America's moral authority', *Business Day*, 23 March 2003.

from an act of war without an enemy nation with which to do battle.'
The inability to respond went to the very heart of the muscular self-
image of the United States.

Something dramatic had to be done to restore that self-image in
the domestic political culture. If the enemy nation did not exist, then
the country that Daniel Boorstin, the American historian, described as
the land of the 'seekers', 'creators' and 'discoverers' had to invent the
enemy nation. And once the enemy nation had been invented there
could be no going back.

A president in desperate need for prestige and gravitas, and a former
army general whose eyes may be set on the highest office in the land,
just could not bear the thought of being cast as 'wimps'. They had to
display that beguiling, all-American leadership quality: 'decisiveness'.
However, while the US has always had a muscular political culture,
the country also exercised its influence through its political, cultural
and intellectual capital. This cultural capital, sometimes known as
cultural imperialism, attracted a great deal of admiration from people
all around the world.

But whenever the muscular image has overshadowed the cultural
image, the US has lost its political and moral authority. The bombings
of Hiroshima and Nagasaki and the war in Vietnam will forever remain
a blemish on American political morality. However, when that muscular
image has been projected in concert with the rest of the world, as in
the war against Hitler, the US has had its political and moral authority
enhanced.

President George Bush in all probability will win the battle against
Iraq but the US will lose the war for global authority – an authority
that can be won and sustained only through the patient cultivation of
consensus among peers.

In its editorial the *New York Times* also described the September
11 bombings as 'the moment in which history splits and we define the
world as "before" and "after"'. But I am afraid that the *New York Times*

may have spoken too soon. The bombing of Iraq may well be that defining moment.

The US has single-handedly provided future terrorists with readymade reasons for reprisals. The global coalition against terror has just been dealt a heavy blow by an inexperienced, impatient American president concerned more with his muscular self-image than the long-term consequences of his actions for the image of his country.

It's a clear case of the tail wagging the dog, as the US gives up its authority in international affairs. Perhaps Bush should ask himself to what extent the following definition of tyrants by Walter Lippmann, America's great writer, applies to his approach to the international community: 'Tyrants are authoritarian leaders, and are in part responsible for the bad odour of leadership among democrats. Custodian only of their own interests, they inculcate consensus by propaganda, maintain it by fear, and defy it when it stands in their way by a seductive terror called charisma.'

The only saving grace is that unlike in tyrannical societies the American public – through elections – have the opportunity to remove the muscular tyranny of George Bush and his gang from world affairs, and thereby reclaim America's authority among the community of nations.

Expanding the meaning of freedom

The 'saving grace' came through the election of Barack Obama as America's first African American president. Now it fell on him to restore America's moral standing in the world. During the campaign Obama often invoked America's founding values by deploying a rhetorical device that is as old as American democracy: 'the promise of America'. In his book *The Story of American Freedom*, Eric Foner describes the contradictory character of American political history thus: 'the contrast between liberty and slavery provided a rhetoric through which those outside the boundaries of American freedom could challenge their exclusion and, in so doing, transform the meaning of freedom itself.' This appeal to the promise of American history goes back to Abraham Lincoln's criticism of the Dred Scott decision, which he assailed as a violation of the Declaration of Independence and its assertion that all men have an inalienable right to life, liberty and the pursuit of happiness. Foner argues that because of their historical experiences black and white Americans looked at freedom differently: 'for whites, freedom, no matter how defined, was a given, a birthright to be defended. For African Americans, it was an open-ended process, a broad, multifaceted concept, a millennial transformation of every facet of their lives and of the society and culture that had sustained slavery in the first place.'[8]

In one of the earliest anticipations of the black consciousness philosophy of self-reliance the great African American leaders Frederick Douglass and Martin Delany argued that those who had known the condition of un-freedom could best describe freedom for America: 'He who has endured the cruel pangs of slavery is the man to advocate liberty.'[9] This expanded notion of freedom was very different from the standard liberal definition of freedom as the condition of being left alone. It was infused with meanings of community as the basis for the dignity of human beings. It is an expanded conception of freedom that has been invoked through the ages right up to Martin Luther King's Poor People's Campaign after the civil rights victory in the 1960s. King pointed to the contradictions of American freedom through a combination of historical and religious rhetoric that had at its heart the idea of the promised land. It is no wonder then that Barack Obama's acceptance of the Democratic Party's nomination was accompanied by images of Martin Luther King. His election

8　Eric Foner, *The Story of American Freedom* (New York: W.W. Norton, 1999), 71.
9　Frederick Douglass and Martin Delany, *The North Star*, 3 December 1847. In *To the Brink* I described how the 19th-century black public intellectual, teacher and minister Tiyo Soga picked on similar line of argumentation about the need for black consciousness in South Africa.

would be a fulfilment of the promise of American history.

Nelson Mandela expressed a similarly expansive conception of freedom in his autobiography, *Long Walk to Freedom*. Whereas Africa's pioneering nationalist leader, Nkwame Nkrumah, had urged Africans to focus on the political kingdom, Mandela was deliberate in linking the political struggle to other social struggles. The fulfilment of the political dream was but a step in the pursuit of the improvement in people's lives. Mandela concludes his autobiography with a chapter aptly titled 'Freedom', in which he argues that political freedom must serve the cause of economic and social justice: 'For to be free is not merely to cast off one's chains, but to live in a way that respects and enhances the freedom of others. The true test of our devotion to freedom is just beginning.' He ends rather poetically:

> I have discovered that after climbing a great hill, one only finds there are many more hills to climb. I have taken a moment to rest, to steal a view of the glorious vista that surrounds me, to look back on the distance I have come. But I can rest only for a moment, for with freedom come responsibilities, and I dare not linger, for my long walk is not yet ended.[10]

The black consciousness leader Steve Biko also had an expansive conception of freedom. Freedom would make possible the exploration of identity. 'We don't behave like Africans, we behave like Europeans who are staying in Africa. So we don't want to be just mere political Africans, we want to be people living in Africa. We want to be called complete Africans.'[11] Elsewhere in his book *I Write What I Like*, Biko provides a definition of freedom as 'the ability to define oneself according to one's own possibilities, held back not by law but by God and natural surroundings'.[12] The idea of freedom

10 Nelson Mandela, *Long Walk to Freedom* (New York: Little, Brown, 1994).
11 Steve Biko, *I Write What I Like* (Johannesburg: Picador, 2004), 148.
12 Ibid., 101.

and development as capability building, which has become vogue in development literature, has long been part of the discourse of black political struggles. This is how Julius Nyerere put it in his classic book *Freedom and Development*: 'people cannot be developed; they can only develop themselves. For while it is possible for an outsider to build a man's house, an outsider cannot give the man pride and self-confidence in himself as a human being. Those things a man has to create in himself by his own actions.'

A word of caution is now in order. With the benefit of historical hindsight we are wiser than to take at face value Douglass's statement that those who have endured oppression are the best guardians of freedom. The best we can say now is: 'it depends ...' Too often those who have endured the cruel pangs of oppression have turned round to visit unbelievable cruelty on others: in the Middle East, in Zimbabwe and in our own bloody history.[13]

Overcoming barriers to expanded freedom at home and abroad

Both Jacob Zuma and Barack Obama have promised to keep open the space for an expanded conception of freedom that focuses on the idea of active citizenship. Both men were the unlikeliest candidates for the leadership of their respective countries. One is an educated black man with a middle name, Hussein, similar to one of America's most hated enemies, who ran for the presidency of a majority white country that is also the most powerful country in the world. The other is an uneducated traditionalist who at one point faced rape and corruption charges in a puritanical society with the most sophisticated economy on the African continent. All the same, the citizens of their countries saw fit to look beyond the prejudices that come with identity politics. But here's the challenge.

13 Xolela Mangcu, Open Letter to Nelson Mandela, *Business Day*, 16 October 2007, and *Sunday Times*, 19 October 2007.

Managing political transitions

Having beaten the electoral odds, the question is whether these leaders will deliver on the promise of their campaigns. All newly elected presidents have to come face to face with the reality of power once they enter government. During the election campaign their party and their supporters are their constituency, but the nature of that constituency is infinitely expanded when they assume office and become leaders of the nation in all its plurality: the rich and the poor, business leaders and workers, investors and the media the world over. What they say and do is under constant scrutiny, and small mistakes are magnified several times over. With their eyes on re-election most presidents tend to lead from the centre.

Barack Obama has not been spared the conservative culture of Washington politics. The hold of what C. Wright Mills called the 'power elite' is something Obama did not fully appreciate in his critique of Harold Washington.[14] The new American president, in order to survive, has to make strategic alliances with these powerful actors if he wants to get his legislative programmes through Congress, particularly those touching the high stakes of international relations, national security and the economy. According to Richard Neustadt, 'the transition perils of newness, hubris, and haste are magnified in the international arena'.[15] Failure to integrate foreign and domestic policy and intelligence can be fatal. The reason why George W. Bush is generally regarded as one of the worst presidents in American history is that, in addition to his hubris, he initiated and presided over a disastrous foreign policy in Iraq, on the basis of what turned out to be flawed intelligence, and all of this within the context of the worst domestic economic crisis since the Depression.

Acutely aware of the dangers of newness, Obama retained the steady hand of Robert Gates as Secretary of Defense, appointed

14 C. Wright Mills, *The Power Elite* (New York: Oxford University Press, 1956).
15 Matthew J. Dickinson and Elizabeth E. Neustadt (eds.), *Guardian of the Presidency: The Legacy of Richard E. Neustadt* (Washington: Brookings Institution Press, 2007).

respected Senator Hillary Clinton as Secretary of State, and picked an economics team that was stronger on experience than innovation, led by Tim Geithner and Larry Summers. He also retained Bush's appointment of Ben Bernanke as chairman of the Federal Reserve. Obama's choices irked many of his supporters on the left wing of the Democratic Party. They argued that these were the very same people who had precipitated the crisis in the first place. But the choices covered the president's right flank. They were meant to counter any perception that the country was in the hands of left-wing novices. Obama learnt well from the experience of Bill Clinton, who had appointed a man with no knowledge of the workings of Washington, Mack McLarty, as his chief of staff.[16]

So how would Obama square his strategic choices with the imperative of bringing a new culture to Washington? Whence would come the innovation he had promised? One answer is that it would come from the White House, from the president himself. That's because at the end of a president's term, there is only one legacy that counts: 'how the President himself – not his vice-president, not his national security adviser, not his secretary of defense, nor any other member of his cabinet or White House staff – has responded to the challenges and opportunities of his times ... the American President ultimately sits alone with history.'[17]

Despite the differences in our political and electoral systems, the same holds for South Africa's leaders. Admittedly, Thabo Mbeki's recall from office demonstrated that South Africa's president occupies his position at the pleasure of the party. But to the extent that individual presidents are the subject of post-presidential evaluations, our presidents too sit alone with history – some being more comfortable with history's judgment than others.

Nelson Mandela is a world historical figure. In 1998 Harvard

16 Harrison Wellford, 'Avoiding the hazards of transition: Neustadt's lessons' in ibid., 72.
17 Ibid., 72.

University held only the third special graduation in its 400-year history in honour of an individual. The first two were the founding president of the United States, George Washington, and Winston Churchill. Mandela was the third, and this is what he said on that day at Harvard Yard: 'To join George Washington and Winston Churchill as the recipient of such an award conferred at a specially conferred convocation is not only a singular honour. It also holds great significance: to the mind and to the future memory of this great American institution, the name of an African is now added to those two illustrious leaders of the Western world.'[18]

By contrast, history will be less kind to Thabo Mbeki. Just as Thomas Jefferson had been privileged to follow Washington and Nehru to follow Gandhi, Mbeki was privileged to follow Mandela. However, he led us on a divergent path which it will take us a long time to retrace before getting our bearings again, for reasons that have been widely documented. Kgalema Motlanthe's time as president was a passing moment, leaving one to wonder whether history will have much to say about his time in office. It was, if anything, a short, safe presidency. He seemed uneasy with power, perhaps a reflection of his self-effacing personality. I remember watching him standing alongside Barack Obama at a G8 photo shoot. 'Say something, anything,' I kept yelling at the television screen. To be sure, Motlanthe made some weighty decisions such as firing Vusi Pikoli as director of the National Prosecuting Authority and allowing the sale of Vodacom shares in Telkom.

There is probably nothing more important to Jacob Zuma than his place in history. For a man who has been persecuted and pilloried as much as he has, there can be no greater satisfaction than history's vindication. As I argued earlier, Jacob Zuma managed the transition rather well, leaving his critics with nothing to say but simply to admire and wonder. He just has to 'keep on keeping on' if he wants to sit

18 Nelson Mandela, Address, *Harvard University Gazette*, 1998.

comfortably with the verdict of history. But this has to be extended to the international front.

Keeping Obama and Zuma honest: the role of active citizenship

While I agree that individuals can shape the course of a country's future, leaving the fate of a country to individual leaders is problematic for at least two reasons. Even the best of presidents have to be pressured to do the right thing. This is simply because it is those who lobby and mobilise for their interests who often get the attention of the president. Civil society organisations need to be on the alert and continually lobby to keep their leader honest and focused on their issues. There is already concern among those who supported Obama that the president has abandoned the theme of community organising that was at the heart of his campaign. In June 2009 I participated in a video conference with leading members of the Obama campaign and administration. The meeting was organised to reflect on how far Obama had gone in making 'active citizenship the central cause of his administration'. The chairman of the Corporation for National and Community Service, Alan Solomont, opened the meeting by highlighting the sea change in the levels of political participation since Obama took over. The administration has created a summer service initiative, United We Serve, to enlist millions in partnership with community organisations to focus on specific community needs, from fixing homes to education. The administration has also succeeded in adopting the Democratic Party's electoral campaign strategy of using new media technologies to engage the public.

But some participants in the video conference were sceptical about the emphasis on community service in the Obama administration. There was an overwhelming sense that the emphasis on service fostered what Harry Boyte called a 'yes we should' as opposed to the 'yes we can' mindset of the campaign. The former treated communities as passive recipients of other people's largesse, while the latter challenged communities to take a more active role in line with what the president had promised. Thus Harvard University's Marshall Ganz – the individual behind the community-organising aspect of the campaign – argued that while philanthropic community service is good, it has nothing to do with citizenship. Citizenship is about achieving equality of voice where there is inequality of resources. Citizenship is a set of political obligations that go beyond volunteerism. One of those obligations is participation in the deliberative life of the community. Ganz concluded by pointing to what Walter Brueggemann called 'the criticality and hopefulness' of the world we live in.[19] Whether we descend into a critical condition or into a world of hope is all our responsibility. While Obama has been leading the charge to change America's image in the world, his ability to lead the world will hinge on his domestic capacity to influence a new generation of Americans to interact differently with the rest of the world, as equal citizens.

Re-examining South African foreign policy

Just as Barack Obama cannot preach active citizenship on the global front without a change in local American culture, Jacob Zuma cannot preach active citizenship at home without changing how South Africa relates to the world. Vusi Mavimbela captured this dynamic in the *Sunday Times* article about political culture referred to in Chapter Two: 'there is a political doctrine which posits that the foreign policy of a country reflects its internal policy, and vice versa. So it can be said that the centrifugal force and the centripetal force pull in opposite directions but have one collective effect in the sense that they both impact upon, and in turn are impacted by, the society we seek to build.'[20]

19 Walter Brueggemann, *The Prophetic Imagination*, 2nd edn (Minneapolis: Fortress Press, 2001).
20 Vusi Mavimbela,'New goals, new strategies', *Sunday Times*, 6 September 2009.

As things now stand, our record in the world is not covered in glory. It does not reflect the long-standing history of a commitment to human rights. Whether we are talking about Thabo Mbeki's or Jacob Zuma's ANC, South Africa has erred on the side of national interest, which is rather ironic given our global status as a country founded on human rights with the most widely acclaimed constitution in the world. But under Mbeki foreign policy reflected a preoccupation with the West. Under his rule we sought to defy the West at every turn, even if that meant providing cover for despots in Burma, Iran, Zimbabwe and Sudan. A former diplomat and director of the Centre for European Studies at the University of Johannesburg, Gerrit Olivier, wrote that Mbeki saw himself as 'Africa's überdiplomat and a world statesman'.[21] Adekeye Adebajo, director of the Centre for Conflict Resolution, argues that South Africa spent a great deal of its time at the United Nations in 'unnecessary spats' with the superpowers over countries which were of no direct concern to South Africa. Adebajo counsels that 'South Africa can only have influence and respect abroad if its leadership is accepted on its own continent'.[22]

I am sure there is a 'feel good' aspect in standing up to the bully and indeed no African leader has done more to bring Africa to the attention of the world than Mbeki. Unfortunately his leadership temperament did more to damage our international public standing than to enhance it. But as far as I can tell, post-Mbeki regimes have swapped one bully for the other – the Americans for the Chinese, if the denial of an entry visa for the Dalai Lama to attend a conference with other Nobel Prize winners is anything to go by. ANC leaders argued that the Dalai Lama's visit coincided with the 50th anniversary of Tibet's rebellion against China and would be seen by China as an

21 Gerrit Viljoen, 'Zuma's modest aims better than Mbeki's lofty goals', *Business Day*, 14 May 2009.
22 In an op-ed article titled 'Time for South Africa's diplomats to get real', *Mail & Guardian*, 8 June 2009.

endorsement of that rebellion. But the real reason was expressed by the government spokesman Themba Maseko: 'We believe that if you have to compare the interests of a peace conference, as opposed to our economic concerns and our bilateral relations, our interests will be better served by making sure we don't jeopardize our relations with China.' The deputy minister of international relations and cooperation, Ebrahim Ebrahim, put it similarly: 'The government did the right thing because, for the first time, our trade relationship with China is positive.'[23]

China is no doubt a powerful country, but as I argued in the following column its democratic credentials and commitment to human rights are still unclear. It makes no sense to jettison or jeopardise our relations with countries with which we have greater historical and cultural affinities such as the United States in order to appease the Chinese.[24]

My friends and I are too old and boring to party. And so between golf games we get together to talk politics. A recent topic was China.

Everyone was going on about China being the next superpower. I spoiled the fun by punching some holes in their arguments. I argued that for all of its promise, China remains a relatively poor country. It may be growing in leaps and bounds, but its economy is a mere fraction of the US.

But I was not finished with them yet. I maintained that the US would keep its advantage for as long as the eye can see because of its ability to invent things – from cars and aeroplanes to electricity, television, the internet, etc.

Then a couple of days ago I was watching an interview with Bill and Melinda Gates on an international news channel. The SABC is so dreary and soapie that I don't bother with their channels anymore.

23 *Sunday Independent*, 26 March 2009.
24 Xolela Mangcu, 'US versus China: I know which side I'm on', *The Weekender*, 28 March 2009.

Bill Gates argued that the global economic crisis notwithstanding, America's higher education institutions were not about to close down their research labs. Microsoft, he boasted, still had a huge research budget. China will not come anywhere near the quality of American higher education in a million years.

So why am I going on about China? Duh? Where have you been these past couple of days? It is completely unbelievable to me – disgraceful is more like it – that a sovereign state can genuflect quite like this to please another sovereign state.

The irony is that the people at the Department of Foreign Affairs have spent the past ten years telling us: 'Africa, define yourself.' The truth is: our foreign policy record sucks!

I have been trying to understand why we continue to find ourselves on the wrong side of international opinion. Yes, I mean Western and American opinion – that is where the financial and intellectual capital will be for a long time.

This may have something to do with liberation history and the influence of the South African Communist Party (SACP). I saw red – literally and figuratively – as soon as Blade Nzimande tried to defend the government's position.

I am reading the book by Stephen Ellis and Tshepo Sechaba's (Oyama Mabandla's nom de guerre in exile), *Comrades against Apartheid*. It's a brilliant read about the SACP's entryism in the African National Congress. This is the idea that the SACP was able to control and influence the ANC by having its most senior leaders, particularly Joe Slovo and Chris Hani, take over senior positions in the ANC. The list of such takeovers is endless.

We have a government that cannot stand up and say, 'Wait a minute!'

We are going from being pawns in the Cold War to being pawns in the duopolistic struggle between the US and China. I know which side I'm on.

In the same newspaper I argued that foreign policy decision-making needs to be subjected to greater scrutiny.[25]

Barring someone from entering your country is such a tasteless thing to do. This is mainly because a government does not own a country. A government is put in power to run a country by the people who actually own the country – that's us.

As columnist Rhoda Kadalie pointed out, what is the point of a government if it is not going to listen to the people? Granted, a government cannot hold a poll every time it has to make a decision. But it also cannot make decisions as if public opinion does not matter. If the government was so sensitive to its Chinese masters, it could have easily allowed the Dalai Lama into South Africa without meeting with him.

We need to find a way in which government decision-making is subjected to greater public scrutiny. Decision-making should not be the prerogative of a few individuals sitting in Pretoria and New Delhi (where the visa was denied).

This rethinking extends to the outmoded notion that a Cabinet minister cannot speak out of step with government. Why not? Will the government suddenly fall? Oh, puh-leeze.

Pursuing human rights through active citizenship: a global agenda

Changing our respective countries' approach to human rights also means changing the language and focus of foreign policy. This involves moving away from the dichotomy between human rights and national interest around which foreign policy discussions pivot. Even though I would like to see a human rights emphasis in our foreign policy, this can best be pursued through an active citizenship approach. Instead of mobilising populations to be their own spokespeople, human rights

25 Xolela Mangcu, 'We, the people, must be heard', *The Weekender*, 28 March 2009.

organisations are too happy to be the guardians of other people, doing very little to empower them. To be sure, these organisations have done a great job in highlighting some of the atrocities taking place around the world, including in Darfur, Sudan. But even in Darfur their overzealousness has led to certain blind spots. According to Columbia University's Mahmood Mamdani, the mere fact that the conflict in Darfur involved Arab Muslims was enough reason to strip it of any political explanation. It became a transhistorical morality tale in which 'the perpetrators are so evil and the victims so helpless that the only possibility of relief is a rescue mission from the outside, preferably in the form of a military intervention'.[26]

I was initially perplexed by Mamdani's response to Darfur and I criticised him in one of my columns for splitting hairs about numbers while people were dying. Was his argument the case of a Muslim defending his own? And yet I knew Mamdani to be much more progressive. But I also confessed to not having read the book. So he called me up and asked me to read the book. Upon reading the book, I saw that there are indeed historical and political precedents to that conflict. According to the historical narrative around which the Save Darfur Coalition coalesced, an immigrant, settler Arab community was committing atrocities against a native African Sudanese population. What Mamdani does rather effectively is to argue that immigration played a marginal role in the making of Darfur and that the conflict was about land between nomads and settled communities. In some cases the conflict was between Arab and non-Arab populations and in some cases among Arab populations themselves. These divisions were manipulated by different sides in the Cold War. At the same time I would simply argue that these political and historical qualifications do not mean that the al-Bashir regime in Sudan is any less murderous, nor do they shield it from international human rights obligations.

I digress, of course. This is not a book about Darfur. The relevance

26 Mahmood Mamdani, *Saviours and Survivors* (Cape Town: HSRC Press, 2009), 67.

of this discussion is the extent to which the complexity of societies is often lost when citizens are not active participants in foreign policy discussions and when public policy is not informed by a study of history. An exclusive focus on human rights as a 'moral' as opposed to a 'political' concept does little to energise populations in different parts of the world. The moral emphasis in international affairs can easily be the equivalent of the service emphasis in domestic policy. Both are necessary but are not sufficient in the development of domestic and international citizenship. Whether it is Thabo Mbeki speaking for the smaller countries of the South or Jacob Zuma seeking to align foreign policy to national interest or the Save Darfur Coalition campaigning against a murderous tyranny, communities become nothing more than beneficiaries of other people's largesse and goodwill – hardly the stuff of political change.

In conclusion, I go back to Marshall Ganz's invocation of Walter Brueggemann's concept of 'criticality and hopefulness'. Individual and collective action will be crucial in expanding active citizenship and curtailing the abuse of power not only in our countries but throughout the world. And that will require building new international alliances to take us from criticality to hopefulness. Just as America and Europe built the North Atlantic Treaty Organisation, there is no reason why America, South Africa and Africa cannot build a transatlantic alliance on citizenship.

8

Conclusion: The next big battle for leadership

I n my previous book, *To the Brink*, I argued that the educated elite can be a threat to democracy. In the present book I have argued that democratic change has not happened because the elite willed it so. Throughout history democratic change has been spurred by the actions of ordinary men and women in response to the specific conditions of their societies. They have often entrusted the leadership of their struggles to the educated elite, while the elite have often turned around to betray their wishes. This book will have succeeded if all it does is demonstrate that South Africa has been no exception to this rule.

Democracy is a historical process that does not come to a halt with the achievement of freedom, and no one can predict for sure which leaders the unfolding of history will give us. I am sure the idea of Jacob Zuma as president of the ANC and as president of South Africa hardly crossed anyone's mind during the liberation struggle. He did not fit the profile of the kind of leader we have come to know since the formation of the ANC almost a hundred years ago. But a particular set of historical circumstances put in motion by his predecessor Thabo Mbeki placed Jacob Zuma at the centre of the historical struggle for the deepening of democracy in South Africa.

Zuma was just as unlikely a candidate for the leadership of South Africa as Barack Obama was for the United States.

At the same time this book will have failed if it elevated these individual leaders above the contradictions of democracy. The problems encountered by their predecessors are not going to disappear because a new group of people are now in charge. Unemployment, inequality, racism, crime and ill health will most likely persist for a very long time. The question is whether our new leaders will deal with these problems with the same defensiveness and denialism of their predecessors or whether they will listen and take seriously what people have to say.

South Africa has had the good fortune of having four presidents in smooth succession in the short span of fifteen years. This is a remarkable feat given that most countries in our continent are often saddled with leaders for decades on end. We have had this leadership succession because our founding leader, Nelson Mandela, believed in the power of historical example. Mandela knew that if he did the right thing, it would reverberate throughout his organisation and lead others to behave likewise. Although Thabo Mbeki sought to extend his stay in power, our political culture would not brook that kind of political behaviour, and he was out of the door before he realised it. His departure led to the election of Kgalema Motlanthe and then Jacob Zuma.

No sooner was the transition from Mbeki to Zuma concluded than the succession debate reared its head again. I almost said 'its ugly head' but succession is not a bad thing. Even if we look askance at individuals seeking to extend their tenure in office into the political future, societies must, if they are to continue to exist, always imagine themselves in the future.[1] People will always ask the questions: Whom can we trust to protect our legacy? Whom can we trust to speak on

1 This concept of how nations imagine themselves in the past and in the future is contained in Benedict Anderson, *The Spectre of Comparison: Nationalism, SouthEast Asia and the World* (London: Verso, 1998).

our behalf? In other words, there are historical reasons why such questions must be asked and why they must be answered. Whether those who provide the answers are driven by power, greed and avarice or are good men and women will depend on the circumstances of each country.

In his book *On Populist Reason*, Ernesto Laclau identifies three moments that characterise populist movements. Firstly, disparate groups, each with their own grievances, emerge in protest against the establishment. At this point the regime can afford to ignore them. Secondly, the groups enter into a coalition or constitute what Laclau calls a populist frontier. Their specific group interests temporarily recede into the background, making collaboration with others possible. Thirdly, no sooner will they have attained power than each constituent member of the coalition will return to its original group position. I shared this insight in a Harold Wolpe lecture some years ago and concluded as follows: 'Once the populist movement attains power the frontier begins to dissolve. This is precisely because the populist frontier – from BEE wannabes to ethnic entrepreneurs to fugitives from the law and the ever-dodgy lumpen – is not an ideologically coherent movement. Wait until Zuma has won, and see the in-fighting that will emerge.'[2]

It is indeed in the nature of political movements in democratic societies to reproduce the outsider–insider dynamic that they themselves protested against. The former outsiders become insiders, and a new set of outsiders is established. This is how the dynamic of democracy is continually created and reproduced. All of a sudden Jacob Zuma the anti-establishment hero becomes Zuma the establishment figure. As Chantal Mouffe puts it, 'a political regime … cannot exist without a constitutive outside.'[3]

It is to this 'constitutive outside' that we must now look to try to

2 Xolela Mangcu, 'Jacob Zuma and the New Politics of Grievance', Harold Wolpe Lecture, 18 June 2007, Cape Town
3 Chantal Mouffe, *The Return of the Political* (New York: Verso, 1993), 152.

understand what the future may have in store for us with regard to leaders. Quite clearly, the South African Communist Party (SACP) and the trade union federation Cosatu are seeking to exert greater influence and control over the direction of the ANC. In an early indication of battles to come, Cosatu and the SACP successfully put their weight behind the election of the high-ranking communist leader Phumulo Masualle as chairman of the ANC in Eastern Cape, arguably the most influential province in the ANC. Recently, the Cosatu general secretary, Zwelinzima Vavi, announced that he would be available for a senior position within the ANC in 2012 and has assured the present secretary-general of the ANC, Gwede Mantashe, that he is not after his job. Vavi cannot contest the presidency because he has repeatedly said that Cosatu would back Jacob Zuma for another term. This leaves open three positions in the ANC: deputy president, chairperson and treasurer. But why would the leader of the biggest trade union federation in the land seek to be merely treasurer of the ANC? This leaves Vavi with two possible options: either to stand for chairman or for deputy president. Taken to its logical conclusion, a 'left' capture of the ANC could see a ticket headed by Blade Nzimande as president, Zwelinzima Vavi as deputy president, and Gwede Mantashe as secretary-general.

Just as many never imagined Jacob Zuma as leader of the ANC or of the country, so we do not know which leaders will be propelled by historical circumstances to lead the battle for the leadership of the country. The businessman Tokyo Sexwale could well still emerge in a frontal challenge to the communist–labour takeover of the ANC. In this he could be joined by the likes of the former ANC Youth League leader Fikile Mbalula and other non-communists within the ANC leadership. Interestingly, both Vavi and Sexwale are agreed that Zuma should serve a second term, which would delay the inevitable duel until 2017. The only person who might have an interest in Zuma serving only one term is Kgalema Motlanthe. After all, he is now the deputy president, and just as Zuma expected to be elevated to the presidency after Mbeki, so Motlanthe might also have such expectations. Moreover, Motlanthe has an influential group of backers in the ANC, particularly in the powerful Gauteng province. But once again he would find himself in the position of caretaker leader, trying to manage the inevitable historical contradictions that lie at the very basis of democracy.

This impossible task is inevitable in a democracy whose fate is tied too closely to the fortunes of one dominant political party. By their very nature political parties want to manage and contain social contradictions – yet democracy thrives on contradictions.

Democratising society

If we are to devolve democracy to society more broadly, then we must also democratise social institutions such as the media and the judiciary, and this means getting them to accept the social and cultural plurality of our society. The patronising and sometimes downright racist manner in which journalists covered the Zuma matter has alienated certain sections of society from the media. One of the most vivid illustrations of this occurred at the ANC's Siyanqoba rally in Ellis Park during the 2009 election campaign. At the beginning of the programme the ANC's Fikile Mbalula asked everyone to sit down so that proceedings could begin. He then instructed members of the media also to sit down – to thunderous applause. It is often argued that so long as people buy newspapers, there is really no reason to change the media. That would be fine if the purpose of the print media is simply to sell newspapers. But if it is to democratise society, newspapers will have to make a greater effort to understand, respect and reflect the plurality and the complexity of the society in which they operate. This may mean not only changing the demographics within newspapers but also improving their understanding of democratic pluralism.

The same sensitivity needs to extend to the judiciary and the development of constitutional jurisprudence. Judge Bernard Ngoepe raised a storm when he suggested that the interpretation of the constitution ought to be grounded as well in the experience of the people in the rural areas: 'Should we go to Washington, Canada or London and ignore as points of reference the values as perceived by, say, tribesmen and women in the rural areas?'[4] This was interpreted as a call for a return to traditional conservatism, which might eventually lead to the reinstitution of the death penalty or a clampdown on the rights of gays and lesbians. The thrust of this book has been that the same holds for politics and the media as well. Eusebius McKaiser quickly responded: 'The worry is that the liberal values that underpin the Constitution are unrecognisable or inherently alien to the majority of South Africans. The implication is that we should undo this "fact". Same-sex marriage, the death penalty and corporal punishment are just some issues that were presumably handled too liberally by the court and which should be reversed.'[5]

Certainly these are false choices. While I agree that our constitutional jurisprudence should not be based on majoritarianism, the alternative cannot be a judiciary that sees its role as a civilising mission existing outside the cultural aesthetics of the society in which it operates. Legal experts have suggested a number of criteria for the selection of judges, such as qualifications, integrity, experience, race and gender. But there is yet another quality which is required of leaders in all sectors of our society. South Africa needs leaders who have been sufficiently exposed to both the world of the elite and that of the masses of people – as much to the ways of Washington, Canada and London as to those of KwaDukuza, Qunu and Soweto. They should have the authority to speak out against the majority when they threaten the values of the constitution and against the minority when

4 Bernard Ngoepe, 'Choosing new custodians of our constitution', *Sunday Times*, 30 August 2009.
5 Eusebius McKaiser, 'The darker side of conservatism', *Mail & Guardian*, 5 September 2009.

they see the people only through prejudiced eyes.

This is the nuanced, deliberative leadership I expect from Jacob Zuma, for as much as he identifies with tradition, he is ultimately a modern political figure.

Index

A

active citizenship 159, 164
  building in SA 165–185
  building in US 165–185
  pursuing human rights through 183–185
  role in keeping leaders honest 178–179
  transatlantic/global alliance on 11, 165–185
African Renaissance 16, 22, 24, 136
amakholwa (educated converts) 7
amaqaba (the red people) 7
ANC (African National Congress) 20, 116
  by-elections in Port Elizabeth 122
  show of strength 124–126
ANC National Executive Committee 62–63, 122
ANC People's War 35, 46
ANC Youth League 58, 155; see also Malema, Julius
Azanian People's Organisation 26, 129

B

Balindlela, Nosimo 41, 116, 122
Biko, Steve 21, 25, 94–95, 102–103,
  108, 110, 116, 144, 166, 173
black commentators 88
Black Community Programmes 22, 24, 156
black consciousness movement/s 24–25, 35, 115, 149, 156–158, 166
black elite 24
black journalists 92
black politicians
  writing about 97–103
Browse Mole Special Report 68
Bus Rapid Transit system 147
business organisations 28

C

cabinet 58
  institutionalising democracy 142–148
  Zuma's selection of 141–148
cabinet ministers 2, 142–148, 183
Calland, Richard 56, 146–147
civic mobilisation 27, 46
civic organisations 27, 46
civic republicanism 17–19
civil society groups 28; see also society
communal reconciliation 23–25
Communist Party 58
  South African (SACP) 2, 45, 182, 189

Soviet Union 45
community agency
   building sense of 156–159
community decline
   in 1980s 25–27
community identity 29
community participation 28
community self–reliance 29
conception/s 33–34
   consumerist, of democracy 31
   consumerist, of development 29, 31
   liberal consumer, of democracy 29
   Mandela's, of reconciliation 24
   of democracy 21
   of freedom 172–173
   of planning 137
   SA's, of development 29
Congress of the People, see Cope
consciousness raising 50, 125, 158
Constitutional Court (CC) 40, 73, 81
   appointment criteria for judges 83
   complaint laid against, by Judge
     Hlophe 76
   media statement by, re Judge Hlophe
     76
   Zuma's appeal to 57, 68
conversation 52, 145, 158
Cope (Congress of the People) 11,
   113–133
   teething problems 118–124
corruption 38, 54, 87, 143, 150
   charges against Jacob Zuma 53–56,
     66, 68, 116, 174
Cosatu 58, 130, 189
crime 38, 87, 143, 157, 187
   Mbeki's view of 88
   of high state officials 8, 71
criminal justice system 10, 39, 73, 82,
   111
Cronin, Jeremy 2–3, 161
cultural aesthetics 107, 191
   of liberal modernity 86, 92, 108
   values 95

cultural insurgency 7, 111
cultural pluralism 111–112
cultural relativism 111

D
De Klerk, F.W. 35, 93, 144
De Lille, Patricia 147–148
deliberative strength 161–164
democracy 35, 38, 42, 53–54, 62, 65,
   84, 90, 95, 131–132, 186, 190
   American 171
   competitive 83
   constitutional 8, 112
   contradictions of 187, 190
   destruction of 73
   devolve to society 190
   dynamic of 188
   formal institutions of 7–8
   history of 35
   in ANC 44
   elite fear of: a historical perspective
     9, 13–31
   evolution of SA's 29
   institutionalising 142–148
   peril that media pose to 106
   principles of 112
   procedural democracy 117
   revival of 3
   substantive democracy 117
   threat of educated elite 186
Democratic Alliance (DA) 78, 118,
   127–128
Democratic Party (DP) 127–128, 169,
   172, 176, 178
democratisation 17, 42
   of society 190–192

E
Ebrahim, Ebrahim 40, 181
economic modernism
   right-wing 138
elections (2009) 126–129
Elephant Consortium 129

elite fear
of democracy: historical perspective
13–31
elite leadership 9
elite politics 7–8
Ellis Park 124–125, 190
engagement 52
Enlightenment rationality 137

F
foreign policy153
re-examining SA's 179–183, 185
US in Iraq 175
freedom 23, 35, 165, 186
American 171–172
authentic 38
Barack Obama's perception of 174
expanding meaning of 171–174
individual 16–17
Mandela's conception of 173
media 87
of association 19
of expression 19, 89, 97–98, 100, 102,
106
of speech 18, 23, 89
overcoming barriers to expanded 174
press 84, 88–89
Steve Biko's conception of 173
Zuma's conception of 174
Freedom Charter 115, 158
Freedom Front 155
Freedom Under Law 78

G
Gear (Growth, Employment and
Redistribution strategy) 138
George, Mluleki 113, 118
governance 5, 7, 21
importance of history in 135–137
governing philosophy
of Zuma 11
Gumede, Josiah 9

H
Hani, Chris 45–46, 48, 118, 154, 182
Harms, Judge Louis 53–54
decision 10
ruling on NPA appeal 66–68
history 10, 18–19, 30, 34, 174, 177
American 140, 148–153, 168–173, 176
ANC 9, 116, 129, 132
as authorisation 115
black social 7, 149
force on civil society 51
government leaders' sensitivity to
159
importance in governance 134–136,
163
importance in policy-making 2, 185
liberation 182
racial 164, 166
Zuma's respect for 139–141
HIV/AIDS 5, 64, 87, 117, 123, 143
Mbeki's policies on 87, 138, 168
Zuma's racialised views on 37
Hlongwane, Mlungisi 116
Hlophe, Judge John 53, 75–77, 85
complaint laid against CC by 76–77
media statement by CC 76
saga of 53
victim of racism 78–82, 84
Hobbes's theory of democracy 14
housing policy
of ANC 28
human rights 180–181
as a moral 185
pursuing through active citizenship
183–185
Human Rights Commission (HRC) 89
inquiry into racism 87–88
international obligations 184
investigation into media 86–88

I
identity politics 126–129, 174
ideological hegemony 46

Idutywa 36, 125
inclusivity 52, 108, 155
Independent Communications
    Authority (ICA) 130
individual reconciliation 23–25
innocence principle 104–105
    as applied to Zuma 93, 103–106
International Criminal Court 169

J
Jafta, Judge Chris 76–77
Jordan, Pallo 40, 45, 48, 95, 101
judicial decisions 72
    consequential for SA democracy
        10, 53
Judicial Service Commission (JSC)
    76–79, 81–83

K
Klaaste, Aggrey 26
Kriegler, Judge Johann 78–80
Kyoto Accord 169

L
law and politics 10, 82
    restoring relationship 71–75
law as politics 53–85
Lazarus, Edward
    on role of judges 72–73
left-wing modernism 138
legitimations 33–34
Lekota, Mosiuoa 37, 49, 69, 95, 113,
    115–116, 118–123
Leon, Tony 65, 127–128
liberal democracy 17, 19–22
liberal modernity 96, 107
    limits of cultural aesthetic 86–112

M
Mabogoane, Meshack 48
Mabandla, Oyama 45, 46, 168, 169, 182
Macozoma, Saki 113, 123
Maduna, Penuell 61, 69–70, 111

Makgoba, Prof. Malegapuru William
    86, 108
Malema, Julius 9–10, 38, 46–50, 63,
    97–98, 116, 119, 147
    example of an underdog 47–50
Mandela, Nelson 20, 35, 114, 118, 125,
    139, 141, 145, 147, 155, 166, 168,
    176, 187
    conception of freedom 173
    conception of reconciliation 24
    father of SA nation 23
    Harvard University honouring
        176–177
    militancy of 9
    reconciliatory gestures 23
    symbolic leadership of 154–155
Mantashe, Gwede 40–41, 97, 99, 147,
    189
Manuel, Trevor 49, 160, 168
Masetlha, Billy 68–69
Mashatile, Paul 143
mass political action 9, 35
mass politics 7–8, 11, 52
Mavimbela, Vusi 51, 179
Mbalula, Fikile 40, 189–190
Mbeki, Thabo 9, 20, 36, 38–43, 48,
    50, 56, 59, 61–64, 66, 71, 82, 87–88,
    92–93, 107–108, 113–116, 139, 148,
    158, 168
    autocratic behaviour 3
    dismissal of 63, 65, 176
    dismissal of Zuma as deputy
        president (2005) 55, 58, 66, 121
    foreign policy under 180
    Harms's ruling 67–68
    high standards of 57
    political conspiracy against Zuma 54
    racial nativism under 44, 108, 119
    rebellion against at ANC's Polokwane
        conf (2007) 37, 42
    sense of history, lack of 136, 139
    suspension of Vusi Pikoli 61
    undermining the RDP 138

Mbokodo 45
McCarthy, Leonard 68, 70, 73, 75
media 10–11, 52, 55, 74, 84–86, 88, 90,
    103, 125, 147, 156, 178, 190
  credibility 89
  freedom 87
  innocence principle 103
  mob psychology about Zuma 99
  offensive examples 42, 97
  racism in 87–90, 108
  role of prejudice in the 91, 106
militarism 9, 44, 133
  as new politics of authenticity 32–52
  revival of 40–43
  violent 94
Mlambo-Ngcuka, Phumzile 113,122
modernism
  high 137, 161
  left-wing 138
  non-racial 27
  right-wing economic 138
Moseneke, Dikgang 40
Motlanthe, Kgalema 37, 41
Mpshe, Advocate Mokotedi 53–54, 82
  decision/s 10
  first decision 58–59
  second decision 68–71, 74–75
Msimang, Judge Herbert 53
  decision 10, 56–58

N
National Housing Forum (NHF) 27–29
National Intelligence Agency (NIA) 68
National Planning Commission 159–
    161, 163
Ndebele, Njabulo 87, 99
NDPP (national director of public
    prosecutions) 10, 40, 54, 61, 67, 74,
    82, 111
New National Party (NNP) 127
Ngcuka, Adv Bulelani 40, 53–54,
    60–61, 70, 73, 75, 113
  decision/s 10, 54–56, 67, 69

Nicholson, Judge Chris 53, 64, 67, 70,
    72
  decision 10, 66
  judgement 59–66, 70
Nkabinde, Judge Bess 76–77
Nolutshungu, Sam 87
non-racial modernism 27
NPA (National Prosecuting Authority)
    57, 60–61, 64, 66, 68–70, 75, 177
NPA Act 71
NPA's appeal 66
Ntsebeza, Dumisa 76, 78
Nyanda, Siphiwe 40, 45

O
O'Regan, Justice Kate 71–72
Oasis Asset Management Company 80
Obama, Barack 139, 163, 165, 167–169,
    171–172, 174,187
  keeping him honest 178–179
  political transition management by
    175–178
  power of symbolic action 148–156
  symbolic leadership 148–156
Omar, Dullah 80
openness 52
opposition parties 11, 119, 128,
    130–131
opposition politics 11
  Cope 129–133
  prospects for 113–133
overarching values 33
ownership 24
  building sense of 156–159

P
Pan Africanist Congress (PAC) 35, 166
People's War, ANC's 35, 46
Phosa, Mathews 41
Pikoli, Vusi 10, 54, 56, 58–59, 61, 177
Pityana, Barney 87, 115, 156
Platform for Public Deliberation 10,
    161

Politburo 45
political authority 33–34, 36
political comeback
    Zuma 58–59
political culture 20, 51, 53, 82, 84, 133,
    141, 144, 179, 187
    domestic 170
    historical contestations of, in SA
        34–40
    intolerant 44
    new 32–34
    of ANC 9, 31, 50
political transitions
    Obama's management of 175–178
    Zuma's management of 175–178
politics as law 53–85
Polokwane conference 37, 113, 122
prejudice in media
    role of 91

Q
Quatro camp 45

R
racial prejudices
    in media 86–11
racism 84, 187
    in Hlophe case 78–82
    in media 86–112
    in US 150–151
Ramaphosa, Cyril 40, 49, 63–64, 78
Ramphele, Mamphela 78, 143, 156
rape charges 98
    against Jacob Zuma 116, 174
Rasool, Ebrahim 41
reconciliation 22
    communal 23–25
    individual 23–25
    Mandela's conception of 24
Reconstruction and Development
    Programme (RDP) 136–138
representative democracy 15–17

S
Sachs, Judge Albie 73
Schreiner, Judge Oliver 67
Scorpions 10
service delivery 23, 29
    crippling concept of 156
    from self-reliant development to
        27–29
    vaunted concept of 131
Sexwale, Tokyo 39, 63, 95, 142, 189
Shaik, Schabir 55–57, 61, 68
Shilowa, Mbhazima 113, 120, 130
Sisulu, Lindiwe 40, 75
Sisulu, Max 40
Sisulu, Walter 48, 110
Skweyiya, Zola 40, 48
Slovo, Joe 45, 80, 182
snob democracy 19–22
social rationality
    vagueness as new 50–52
society 25–26, 39, 49, 90, 93–94, 103,
    118, 126, 136–137, 149, 158, 172
    civil 13–14, 28, 51, 112, 133, 147,
        153, 178
    democratising 4, 157, 190–192
    industrialised 7
    pluralistic 112, 133, 190
    plurality of 31
    political culture of 32
    prejudices of 84
    psyche of civil 51
    puritanical 174
    racially polarised 23
    racism of 84
    role of press in 89
    welfarisation of 30
    Western values 103
South Africa 11, 186
    beginning of snob democracy in
        19–22
    building active citizenship 165–185
    cultural affinities between African
        Americans and SA 165

democratic competition 124
development in 29
evolution of democracy in 29
foreign policy re-examination 179–
183
jurisprudence 71
liberalism in 110–111
political culture, history of 34–40
presidency 7
race relations in 116
two strands of democracy in 17
South African Communist Party
(SACP) 45, 182, 189
South African Institute of Race
Relations 109
Squires, Judge Hillary 55–56
Steyn, Douw 87
struggle 15, 29, 34, 139, 167–168,
173–174, 186
armed 35, 166
credentials 96–97, 102
normative 89
of poor 52
rise in 1980s 25–27
Supreme Court of Appeal (SCA) 57,
66, 76
Suttner, Raymond 44, 46
symbolic action
power of 148–156
symbolic leadership 160
Mandela 154–155

T
taxi owners 147, 162
technocracy
undermining historical imagination
136–139
Thales/Thint 54, 57
trade unions 30
transatlantic/global alliances 11
towards active citizenship 165–185
transition stages 36–40
Truth and Reconciliation Commission

(TRC) 23
Tshwete, Steve 45, 111

U
ubuntu 24
Umkhonto weSizwe (MK) 45
umrabulo (consciousness raising) 50
underdogs 30–31
culture of 31
Julius Malema as example 48–50
United Democratic Front (UDF) 26
United States (US) 11, 15, 51, 161, 163
building active citizenship 11,
165–185, 187
discrimination against black people
89
links with SA 164
role of history in governance 140,
148–154, 168–173, 176

V
vagueness
as new social rationality 50–52
Vavi, Zwelinzima 46, 97, 99, 189
violence 13, 26, 49, 65, 133, 166
interminable racial 20
spectre of 44–47
types of 46
victims of 26
xenophobic 47, 142
violent rhetoric action 9

W
Washington, Harold 160–161, 163, 165,
175
power of symbolic action 148–156
symbolic leadership 148–156
welfarisation
of society 30
white journalists 87, 96, 100

X
Xingwana, Lulu 143

Xundu, Mcebisi 156

Z
Zanempilo Health Clinic 156
Zille, Helen 78, 96, 130, 148
Zimbabwe 38, 63–64, 87, 103, 117, 174, 180
Zuma, Jacob 49, 66, 69–70, 72, 83
    and ANC 139
    and militarism 44
    appeal against confiscation of documents 56–57
    appeal against Mpshe's charge 59–60
    controversies around 116
    corruption charges against 53–56
    criticisms about 146
    governing philosophy 11
    Judge Hlophe's matter 76–77, 82
    keeping him honest 178–179
    non-ideological 50
    political comeback 58–59
    political transition management by 175–178
    populist coalition 51
    racist writings on 92–112
    respect for history 139–142
    SCA finding on NPA's appeal 66–68
    selection of new cabinet 142–148
    state's actions against 73–75

Other titles from Jacana

Native Nostalgia
by Jacob Dlamini

The Poverty of Ideas:
South African Democracy and the Retreat of Intellectuals
edited by William Gumede and Leslie Dikeni

Zumanomics:
Which Way to Shared Prosperity in South Africa?
edited by Raymond Parsons

The Mail & Guardian A-Z of SA Politics
edited by Rapule Tabane and Barbara Ludman

Zunami!
The South African Election of 2009
edited by Roger Southall and John Daniel

Inside Quatro:
Uncovering the Exile History of the ANC and SWAPO
by Paul Trewhela

The ANC Underground in South Africa to 1967
by Raymond Suttner